OPEN

WIDE

OPEN

DR. MARK MANHART'S JOURNEY
IN DENTISTRY, THEATRE, EDUCATION,
FAMILY, AND LIFE / **A BIOGRAPHY**

WIDE

LEO ADAM BIGA

Omaha, Nebraska

ISBN13: 978-1-936840-80-9
LCCN: 2011937597
Cataloging in Publication Data on file with publisher.

Calcium Therapy Institute Press
Omaha, Nebraska
www.CalciumTherapy.com

Printed in the United States
10 9 8 7 6 5 4 3 2 1

CONTENTS

1

A Life in the Open

We all lead a few lives or, if you prefer, double lives.

Mark Manhart knows something about the mirrors of life. In his professional life, he is a dentist. In his personal life, he is a writer, director, history buff, landscaper, father, grandfather, and husband among a few different pursuits.

"I think everybody has that kind of dual life going, especially people who get into such specialized things as dentistry. A professional has to lead two lives. Your open life and your other lives," he said.

The Omaha, Nebraska resident has an opinion on most everything, and he usually has a philosophy to support his viewpoint. Try this one on for size: "One needs a real work-a-day life and then at least one other life, some hobby, avocation, distraction, to work on to nearly inane proportions, so one can return to home base refreshed, go to bat again, and make your way before the inning and game is played out. I have gone through many family and professional things that were very much like sitting in the dental chair. All have been adventuresome."

For this man of many interests and talents, life is also full of what he likes to call "natural wonders"—those unforgettable people and events that he enjoys experiencing and cultivating. He is all about opening new horizons of discovery in his personal and professional lives.

One domain feeds the other; one dimension offers solace from the other. "All of this, in any position or occupation, is terribly important to one's sanity, pleasure, growth, and accomplishment," is how he sees it.

For fifty years Manhart has indeed left the confines of home for the office, leaving behind his domestic incarnation for that of the highly trained, working professional who not only practices dentistry but is actively engaged in developing new treatments or therapies.

Then there is the life that revolves around some inner passion that enables him to return to work recharged, ready to resume life in the open and persevere. For Manhart, it is the world of arts and letters that feeds or fulfills him with the sustenance to carry on with renewed vigor. Specifically, it is the life of the theatre and his work as a playwright and director, and occasionally as an actor, that is a source of satisfaction, of solace, of energy, of intellectual and emotional discovery that offers a balance or complement to his professional and family endeavors.

There is also the life he maintains with his spouse. Here, too, Manhart is well-versed in that song and dance called marriage. He has been married twice. His first marriage lasted more than two decades and resulted in eight children. That union ended in divorce, but when he was ready to start a new chapter in his life, he did not hesitate to marry again, to a woman with a pair of children of her own. This second marriage-go-round has now exceeded more than two decades itself, which would seem to indicate he is the marrying kind.

Bonnie and Mark, circa 2005

He and his wife, a spitfire named Bonnie Gill, make it work despite being very different personalities. They may not see eye to eye on many things, and they may handle situations quite differently, but when it comes to what is important in life, they are simpatico. They are both searchers, ever inquisitive to turn the next page in life, to see what is over the next hilltop, to experience a new culture or way of doing things. Both are principled people. Both would rather give than take. Both are creative souls.

It seems Mark Manhart's thirty-year dental partnership with Dr. Tom Steg can be thought of as a kind of marriage in itself. The two men are opposites in most ways but are kindred spirits where it counts most, as people of high character, intense curiosity, extreme professionalism, and with a penchant for pushing beyond the norm of dentistry to find the best ways of caring for patients.

With his tall frame, angular features, shock of silver hair, confident pose, resonant voice, formal manner, and reserved personality, Manhart cuts a striking, classic figure. He comes across at once as a bold, magnetic personality with an authoritative air and yet at the same time as a quiet, pensive, somewhat shy, even insecure soul. It is that duality that is so much a part of him. It is an expression of his charm and his complexity.

Call it fate or coincidence, but this practitioner of the healing art of dentistry also became a creative artist somewhere along the line. More likely, he was an artist right from the start and his muse simply waited for when the time was right to finally bloom. Many of the qualities that make up a healer, after all, are much the same as those that characterize an artist: empathy, discernment, problem-solving, discipline, craft, even imagination.

Manhart still lives that personal brand, striking a balance between right- and left-brain activities that put him squarely in the mix of Omaha culture, community, and commerce. Long before social networking became a catch-word and lifestyle for the online era, he was engaging people from all walks of life and exploring ideas from disparate sources.

He was ahead of the curve on the Internet as well, launching a website for his practice back in 1995. He is on LinkedIn, Facebook, and all the other go-to social media sites. He blogs. He even conducts online training sessions for dentists from around the globe. He is as connected as anyone of his generation.

His inclusive, progressive approach to dentistry may best illustrate how open-minded and receptive he can be to new ideas and new collaborators. Eager to always improve his craft, he makes a habit of seeking out the latest advances by poring over dental journals from around the globe. Staying current this way has spurred him to make his own breakthroughs and to share his advancements with peers in the United States and abroad.

Away from dentistry, his work as a playwright and theatre director reflects his eclectic tastes, ranging from sentimental love stories to historical dramas to bawdy comedies to high-brow treatises to full-blooded biographies to English manor mysteries. From kitsch to classic, Manhart embodies it all.

Not so very different from the way he seeks to break new ground in dentistry, he actively seeks out new forums and challenges in theatre. He has done the same in education, too, as a champion for the Montessori method of early childhood instruction and for home-schooling. Although he has been a clinician most of his working life, he has also taught dentistry formally at the university level and informally in workshops and trainings.

Whether navigating the worlds of medicine, business, education, or art, he is an enterprising, energetic innovator open to new, even unconventional ways of doing things. He is what some people call today "a creative." It is really another word for "eccentric" or for how one of his own children described him—"a half bubble away from genius." That missing other half of the effervescent bubble can sometimes make him look like a fool or an idiot some people very close to him will tell you. It is a risk he is willing to take.

His work and life are expressions of an inquisitive mind and a sensitive disposition. His office displays pictures of the charming digs he kept in The Passageway of Omaha's historic Old Market district, the cultural heart and soul of the city he felt right at home in. Once the wholesale produce center for the city, the district was redeveloped beginning in the late 1960s and early 1970s into a European-style marketplace.

The Mercer family of Omaha led efforts to preserve and reuse the century-old warehouses as restaurants, galleries, theaters, shops, and residences. Manhart fit right in with the Old Market's creative class denizens.

The Old Market has become one of the state's largest tourist attractions, along with the world-class Henry Doorly Zoo as a magnet bringing visitors to the city. Due to health issues of his own, Manhart long ago had to set aside this second office in The Passageway at 10th and Howard Streets. The Market and his affection for that Old World location is evident in the photographs he displays of the brick-hewn office and environs he practiced in there. He also keeps an antique dentist's chair in his West Omaha office as a token of his appreciation for "good old-fashioned" dentistry, craftsmanship, and values.

Manhart's full life is not just a professional or aesthetic exercise. His life extends to family. He came from a huge clan, and he is the father of eight himself.

"I always wanted a large family of twelve children. A lot of kids who could become 'adult' adults. As a granddad, it is hard to see much success in that regard, so I must wait it out. I think I was a good father but that is slightly biased. People would say I am too harsh, too outspoken, too busy elsewhere, distracted too easily, too liberal, too persistent, frugal to cheap, an exaggerator, cold with little emotion, a trouble starter, and more. An old friend, a Jewish lady, hit it for me: 'You are a starter. We have enough finishers.' My obligation to the kids was to house, feed, protect them from others and each other in a way that they would be able to do the same as adults, and love them. Most of the love was, and will remain, secret between each one and me. Some day I want to write about that," he said.

Cast members of plays from Great Plains Theatre Conference

Those who know Manhart from his life in the arts may not even know he is a family man, much less a dentist. Just as those who identify him as a dentist may not be aware of his other lives. That is all par for the course for someone who throws himself passionately into whatever endeavor he is engaged in at the moment. It is not as though he focuses on a passion to the outright exclusion of everything else, but he does tend to lose himself in whatever it is he is engaged in at the moment.

His single-minded devotion is evident in his dental career. He has been in private practice now forty-five years. Counting his time doing dentistry in the United States Air Force Dental Corps and his time in dental college, he has been actively engaged in the field of dentistry for more than half a century. However, the way he has chosen to practice, by utilizing noninvasive calcium treatments of his own design, has made him an outcast of sorts within his field. And being shunned by the dentistry establishment was just the beginning; legal action to stop him followed, but each case served to strengthen his resolve.

To further his somewhat nontraditional approach to dentistry, he founded and directs the Calcium Therapy Institute in his hometown of Omaha. The Institute is the vehicle for Manhart to do dentistry and science side-by-side, using his preternatural inquisitiveness and idiosyncrasy to investigate dental problems and treatment options along lines that do not necessarily conform or adhere to organized dentistry's prescribed ways. That is just the way he likes it, too. Tweaking the nose of authority is a Manhart trait.

He enjoys playing the contrarian. Much the same way his late father, a farmer-turned-attorney-turned-inventor, was his own man who went his own way, damn the consequences, Manhart is a maverick accountable only to himself. He takes the road less traveled, whether in his personal or professional affairs, following an inner muse that neither brooks compromise nor suffers fools gladly nor worries about what people say.

There have been times when he has severed major threads in his life in order to do what he felt was right, regardless of how others perceived him and his decisions. For example, he and his first sweetheart, Mary, married and raised a large family together. She is the mother of his eight kids. After the kids were grown, the couple decided to end the marriage.

"Mary and I were happily married for a long time," he said. Then they simply reached a place in time when they determined they would be better off apart.

Following years as an active member of the American Dental Association and officer in the ADA's Omaha branch, he set aside organized dentistry as well. He has practiced without direct affiliation with the dental establishment— that is, his ADA membership and a position teaching at his dental school. However, the tradeoffs became more focused on his patient care, clinical research, and life beyond dentistry. At the time he won a lawsuit over patient treatment that was egged on by dentists who opposed his research in the advanced uses of calcium materials. When a number of specialists testified against him, there were subsequent, immeasurable losses to his reputation and health.

Aside from getting some of his findings published in *the* preeminent international dental journal more than twenty-five years ago, and in a few minor journals, his attempts to publish his work in America have been repeatedly rebuffed, much to his frustration. Nonetheless, in 2009 a prestigious European dental journal published his latest findings almost immediately and without reservation. His perceived banishment in the United States is a source of bitterness with him but just how much it bothers him is hard to gauge as he tends to dismiss it or brush it aside as no big deal. His wife, Bonnie, knows differently.

How much has he been hurt by all this? "Very hurt. More than you can imagine," she said. "I cannot even talk to him about it, and some of it I think he has brought on himself. But I think as he gets older it is killing him and I keep telling him, 'You gotta let it go.'"

Bonnie said her husband can be hard to read, even for her, because he is such a mix of things and because he can hide behind an inscrutable, sphinx-like mask that serves to insulate and isolate him from those around him.

"I know him probably better than anybody else, I would say better than any human being on Earth," she said. "He is a very complicated soul and a very kind person. It is sometimes the bane of his existence and actually what probably drew me to him. I knew before I ever got hooked up with him that he was incredibly honest. What I do not admire is that he can seem to turn that on and off and be extremely cruel when he wants to be, too. This is one of his flaws—it's my way or no way—he cannot ever see the gray areas on some of this stuff, which he is very good at seeing on other things."

11

She has no trouble standing up to him when she feels he is wrong and telling him so. He can handle being called out on his mistakes and has no problem with Bonnie's candidness and her telling him like it is.

Bonnie said, "You know, it takes a pretty strong guy to accept being told, 'I think you're full of it.' But that is the kind of relationship we have. It's perfect because I do not ever have to get up wondering who I should be today." In other words, she can be herself. With Mark," she said, "I always know I can be who I am, warts and all, and it might be a little grumpy, but it's going to get worked out."

She has been there through the highs and lows of his dental life. She has seen the toll it has taken on him to seek the kind of vindication and recognition he wants but that has not been forthcoming and that likely will not come anytime soon, much less in his lifetime. "One time I asked Mark in the throes of this, 'Do you want to be rich or do you want to be famous?' And I did not even have to ask him because I knew what the answer was. He threw me a curve ball though by saying, 'Both.' I said, 'You cannot have both, you can only have one.' And then he said, 'Famous,' and I said, 'I knew that.'"

Despite setbacks he has doggedly carried on, determined to prove people wrong. Call him intransigent or stubborn or willful or simply determined, he is like the proverbial dog that won't give up a favorite bone without a scrap. As stressful and contentious as his dentistry battles have been, the bulk of his work in the field has been fulfilling. It is why he still does what he does at an age when the vast majority of his peers are long retired.

"Look at when dentists retire. I mean, dentists retire pretty darn early, and I passed that opportunity up fifteen years ago. I keep on because our calcium therapy works and it is such a delight to practice dentistry," he said. "You know every day I see people who have troubles and we solve them. What more of an ego trip could you want?"

A pursuit quite apart from dentistry that Manhart is no less passionate or obstinate about is the theatre. This dramatic arts enthusiast has taken the hobby seriously enough to have helped form and operate three community theatre venues: the Rudyard Norton, the Kingsmark II, and the Grande Olde Players (GOP). He co-founded and directed the latter with Bonnie. Their Grande Olde Players established a niche by producing works featuring seniors and intergenerational casts. After a twenty-four year run the Grande Olde Players Theatre, which also featured jazz concerts, staged its final season in 2008.

Manhart has also participated in the Great Plains Theatre Conference hosted by Metropolitan Community College. The college's historic Fort Omaha campus is the site of play labs where Manhart's work has been read and where he and Bonnie have directed play lab readings of works by other playwrights. The conference receives submissions from playwrights across America, even from abroad. It is an intensive week-long concentration on craft. Some of theatre's greatest talents participate as readers, respondents, mentors, and panelists, all in service of furthering the work of new and emerging playwrights.

Manhart does not kid himself. He knows he is not in the same league as many of the participants, who have included Pulitzer, Tony, and Obie award winners. The experience of having his work critically evaluated has not discouraged him but has emboldened him to keep writing and improving.

He has already accomplished much in local theatre. Without a lick of formal training he taught himself how to write, produce, cast, and direct productions and to manage theatre companies. He still writes plays and he still takes directing assignments today. Bonnie also continues to write and direct. Much like his experience in dentistry, he has often butted heads with theatre colleagues and collaborators, but, right or wrong, he has always remained true to himself, which is that of a stubborn, "tough old German," as he likes to say with a wry smile. He is actually Swiss and German, with a little French thrown in, although the borders of those countries changed so often in the not-so-distant past that his precise lineage on his father's side, the German side, cannot be determined with absolute certainty. On his mother's side, the Swiss side, however, the family line can be traced back some eight hundred forty years.

The worlds of dentistry and theatre could not be more unalike on the surface. But look closer and what at first seems incongruent reveals similarities, which is why Manhart has drawn from each to enrich the other. Of course, when you think about it, dentistry entails a performance aspect. After all, the practitioner fulfills the role of expert healer for the patient, who comes in search of relief. The drama and expectation alone make it a kind of theatre. Conflict is at the heart of any drama and the inherent conflict in the doctor-patient relationship is that the healer may have to cause the patient discomfort, even pain, before healing occurs.

For many patients the mere thought of going to the dentist produces extreme anxiety. Sitting in the examination chair, surrounded by all that cold, hard, sterile equipment, which for all the world resembles instruments of torture, is enough to raise anyone's blood pressure. Then there is the whir of the drill. Add to that the unpleasant past experiences many have had in a dental office, from scrapings to extractions to injections, and you have the makings for a tense situation.

Then there is the often exorbitant cost of dentistry that not all patients have the insurance to cover. The financial burden of care is a source of some resentment. It is routine nowadays for a few extractions or a root canal, for example, to cost many hundreds of dollars. When you talk about bridges, crowns, and implants, the bill ratchets up into the thousands. Finally, some doctors do not exactly have a winning chairside manner with their condescending, paternalistic I-speak-you-listen, I am-the-expert-you-are-the-patient attitude.

In stark contrast to that dysfunctional model, Manhart goes out of his way to provide high-quality service at a reasonable rate and to deal with patients in a respectful manner that makes them a part of the care plan. He has also refined his craft to the point that his supple hands have a sure touch. He said there are qualities, some tangible, some intangible, that separate a master practitioner from a run-of-the-mill one.

"It is their touch, their approach, their finesse, whatever you want to call it," he said. As a young dentist he had a chance to not only see but to feel some masters at work. "I thought, there is the kind of practitioner I would like to be." By all accounts, he has become one. He said, "My rule always has been, man, if I can get my hands on you, you will never go anywhere else."

Such finesse only comes through an assurance and confidence that cannot be approximated or faked. You either have it or you don't. "That's everything, yeah," said Manhart. "You cannot really hide it. It's there and it's in everything you do. I worked for an orthodontist named Dr. Elmer Bay, and as a teacher this guy was absolutely wonderful because you never knew you were being taught. I used to make his appliances for orthodontics, and I saw his superlative results in everything. He was very old-fashioned. A few years ago Dr. Steg [Manhart's dental partner] said to me, 'I had a patient who was told by so-and-so she should not go to us because we are old-fashioned dentists.' Well, that is the best compliment anybody has ever given us because those old-fashioned dentists like a whole lot we grew up with were just wonderful."

One old-time dentist Manhart worked with, Dr. Leo Ripp, was so well-loved and appreciated that at his funeral mourners eulogized what a great dentist he was. Manhart never heard of such a thing. "Old Dr. Ripp, he could make the most beautiful gold crown you could ever believe seeing with the oldest crap you could ever think of using," he said. "He really just was superb. He would put a crown in someone's mouth, and if it did not stay forty years, something was wrong here."

Manhart has the utmost respect for the men who taught him because they were working dentists. They were the first practitioners and second teachers he has tried emulating.

"Most of my training was given to me by dentists who were practicing fulltime and coming in a little bit each week and teaching. That kind of dentist is a clinical, hands-on dentist. They really know what is going on. But since the middle 1970s or somewhere in there, the dental school faculties have been dominated by fulltime teachers who go to practice a little bit and that changes the whole picture. That changes it even in the sense of the patient-dentist relationship. When you are working on your own patients and you are listening to them, you are really listening to them, number one, and you are making decisions together, number two, and you know little things like if this patient is not happy, they are going to go home and tell seventeen people. Now you either make them happy or you are in big trouble," he said.

Conversely, he said a sense of accountability tends to be in shorter supply among dentists who teach fulltime because in college dental clinics dentists are not seeing their own patients, they are seeing whoever walks in for treatment, and these patients are apt not to get the same attention they would in a private setting. From where Manhart sits, too, there is something to the old adage, "Those who can, do, and those who can't, teach." Therefore, let the buyer beware.

In such a setting, he said, the dentist tends to be insulated from any repercussions that attend substandard care. A gulf or separation existing between dentist and patient is not consistent with quality care. He feels this insularity is engendered, too, in some dentists who belong to the American Dental Association, who use the organization as a buffer. "That insulation makes you act differently," he said. Less compassionately or less empathetically perhaps. Rather than hide behind an association, Manhart puts himself right out there, taking full ownership of who he is and what he does. "When you go onto the Internet—this is the first thing I found out—you open yourself up to the entire world and a lot of dentists cannot allow themselves to do that," he said.

Furthermore, Manhart strives to do the most for his patients with the least overhead for fancy equipment. He has developed an array of techniques, products, and applications that treats patients in minimally invasive or entirely noninvasive ways that are also quick and painless. He is efficient enough to get patients in and out of his office in short order but without resorting to shortcuts or rushing through procedures. That is because he has reduced procedures from several steps to just a few steps, eliminating waste, excess, and overkill. Yet he still takes time to actually examine the inside of the patient's mouth, explain things, ask questions, and lay out options. He is all about finding long-term solutions, not quick fixes. It is the way informed consent is supposed to work, he said.

Arlene Nelson has been a patient of his for nearly forty years, and she appreciates his inclusive approach. "He shows me the X-rays every time. He says, 'I want you to look at this.' He just explains things to you and you just get a clear picture of what is going to be done and how long it is going to take and how many treatments or whatever. You feel like you are a part of the improvement. You really are, too. He puts you right in there. You are right there and you are a part of the healing process. He gives you an ear-by-ear, side-by-side walk with the healing," she said. "He has really done me right. I have just been very pleased. He is very gentle, very sure."

His old-fashioned approach is something she appreciates. "You know, I kind of like that. Not only that, but I had a tooth that was bothering me that was way in the back, and I actually called him at home on a Sunday and he said, 'I want you to meet me at the office at one o'clock,' and I did. I did not ever think I would be calling a dentist at home. It turned out he had someone flying in from wherever for treatment that day. I thought, oh my gosh. He is just so ready to help me. He is my kind of dentist."

Paul Luc appreciates the holistic way Manhart treats dental problems. A Hong Kong native living and working in Tennessee, he is typical of Manhart's patients from all over the country, even all over the globe, who have discovered the Calcium Therapy Institute (CTI) via the World Wide Web. Dozens more do every day.

Diagnosed with advanced periodontal disease, Luc studied the CTI website, contacted Manhart, and arranged to come to Omaha for a treatment. People from coast to coast and from overseas venture in every other week. Like so many of Manhart's patients, Luc came to the Institute after "seeing and consulting with a variety of general dentists and periodontists ... the options offered to me were not satisfactory. The mainstream approach may be clinically acceptable, but it is too generic and statistical in nature and not patient-oriented," said Luc, who is a scientist. "I was searching for a holistic dentist. The trip was everything I had hoped for and more. Dr. Manhart's approach is entirely patient-oriented. His method of treatment and diagnosis is very practical, realistic, and above all very scientific. There was no pain, no surgery, no blood, no X-ray, and no anesthesia. Within twenty-four hours after the initial treatment, my condition was under control. It improved drastically after two more days of intensive treatment."

Luc found Manhart's "genuine concern" encouraging. He also appreciated that Manhart was willing to share his immense knowledge with him, patiently answering his many questions and offering him the best options for his particular needs. Like more and more CTI patients, Luc uses several of its self-care products at home, including the Calcium Toothbrush, the Oral-Cal mouthwash, and the Calcium Chip set. "My gums and teeth are getting better every day. I am really amazed by the power and effectiveness of the simple, common sense approach and solution."

There is more to the story. Luc was so taken by the results that he began focusing his scientific mind on a practical application for determining the presence of periodontal disease. Long story short, Luc devised a home test that he then presented to Manhart, who immediately saw that his patient had hit upon something worth developing.

"Paul came up with a superb test for periodontal disease," he said. "It is very neat. He adapted our products in a certain way so that you test yourself at home to tell whether you have periodontal disease or anything to worry about with your gums being infected. Paul is very creative, and he came up with a very clever oxidase process for testing. All I did was tweak it and put it in a sequence of what to do. If we had some company to work with, it could be made very inexpensively with materials we have."

A doctor being open to accepting an idea from a patient is rare enough. It shows that Manhart is not so high and mighty as to dismiss something a mere civilian suggests or, in this case, invents. He has too often been on the other side himself of being cast as the amateur or dilettante intruding into the holy domain of the experts or specialists. So he knows what it is like to be ridiculed and spurned and not taken seriously. He has a long history of being open to ideas from many quarters.

In September 2009 he and Bonnie were presenting the calcium therapies in Nice, France, when one of the attendees answered the following question Manhart posed: "What causes such an infection?" To which a man in the audience responded with, "Thumb sucking." Manhart, the expert dentist, was bewildered that he had never thought of that explanation.

In his practice Manhart must be a people-person and thus he can turn on the charm and therefore transform the often awkward patient-doctor interaction into a relaxed exchange that disarms patients and makes them collaborators in their own care. Humility goes much further than arrogance he has learned. But with him, there is no ring of phoniness to the interaction. He is genuinely engaged and in the moment with you. You feel his full attention on you.

"I always remember how theatre helped me become a better dentist, because you have to play a role," he said. "If you go into the office and play the role of a student, people do not buy it. If you cannot play the role of a dentist who is competent, who knows what the hell you are doing even though you maybe have to go in your office and read a little to make sure you know what you are doing, then you are going to fail at it. And it works the other way, too. You learn things on stage that work and make sense that can be applied to your dental work, and one of them for me was that we were always taught in dental school never to say things like, 'Ooops' or 'Sorry, I didn't mean to cut your lip off.' You were taught to be impervious to mistakes. Well, it is an everyday thing because you are hurting people every day, and so how do you respond?

"I remember we were taught you never give a person an injection and say, 'I'm sorry.' That is heresy or it used to be, maybe it is not so much anymore. I just figured out, no, I have to say that, and so it has gotten to be a habit with me. Almost every time I give someone an injection and I know I have hurt them, I have to say, 'I'm sorry,' and it has to be real. That makes a person a better dentist, just simple empathy. Otherwise, it is not believable."

Just as he has learned that genuineness is a big part of being a healing arts practitioner, he has learned it is equally critical to being an artist on the stage. In each circumstance it is about transparency and professionalism. It is all about being authentic or real. Anything less than that will not hold or convince the audience. People can smell a phony act from a mile away.

He has taken his ability to authentically, transparently engage people a step further by devoting much time to teaching his craft. For four years he was an associate professor at his alma mater, Creighton University Dental School in Omaha. One of his former students, Tom Steg, is now his partner. The two make an interesting contrast. Manhart is the tall, thick figure whose bigger-than-life vibe and presence draws eyes to him. Steg is a slight man with an insular personality and a just-above-a-whisper voice. But where they differ outwardly they share the same probing intellect that enjoys the give-and-take of rigorous inquiry.

Manhart in *See How They Run*

For years, Manhart has demonstrated techniques to colleagues at dental conventions across America, even abroad. At various times he conducts seminars for dentists in his office or their offices, turning the quarters into teaching labs where he works on actual patients while dentists and hygienists observe. His work as a clinician-teacher is widely respected because he is not only skilled and informative but knows how to play to the crowd and work a room. He makes eye contact, he changes the inflection of his voice, he pauses for effect, he gestures with the tools of his trade in his hands. Like any good actor or orator, he uses his entire body and whatever props are available as expressive instruments of communication.

Being able to "perform" in front of people when the pressure is on is a knack he developed early on in competitive athletics and refined as a dentist and later in Rotary International and community theatre. The Rotary International website's "About Us" section describes itself as "the world's first service club organization, with more than one million members in thousands of clubs worldwide. Rotary club members are volunteers who work locally, regionally, and internationally to combat hunger, improve health and sanitation, provide education and job training, promote peace, and eradicate polio under the motto Service Above Self."

Sounds like a hand-to-glove fit for Manhart, the man of varied interests, especially when the Rotary site gets around to the part that says "the benefits of a Rotarian include serving the community, networking and friendship, and promoting ethics and leadership skills." That is Manhart to a tee. He can and did hold his own with Omaha movers-and-shakers when he was active in Rotary. He is not so much active in it anymore, but he still follows the organization's principles in his private and professional lives.

He suffered stage fright during his first forays in theatre but interacting with patients and with peers as a dentist and getting up and addressing an audience at Rotary meetings helped instill a composure that he then transferred to the stage. In turn, he took what he learned in theatre and applied it to his profession, especially to the public speaking, demonstrations, and teaching he does. "It taught me in a way how to present myself in giving a clinic or giving a lecture. It taught me that talent," he said.

He remembers the first time he ever went and presented anything in Chicago, host of *the* dental convention in America. He said, "It is like being on the best stage in dentistry, it really is," and how much smoother and assured he was in that rarefied environment after honing his public speaking and theatre chops. He likes being on stage, whether in the playhouse or the examination room or the classroom or the convention hall. His hands are sure, his voice steady, his posture erect, and his demeanor confident in these respective arenas. Each is a turf he feels completely comfortable and competent on.

He transferred this same nonplused quality to local cable television, for which he wrote, directed, and hosted talk shows that produced some one hundred programs featuring guests from all walks of life. He developed and hosted a talk show on Omaha's KLNG Radio for a time. He has also appeared in a number of local TV and radio commercials. The ham in him cannot help it. Besides, he is just one of those high-energy people, as is Bonnie, who has to be doing something.

Add to that his boundless curiosity, his stage presence, and his gift for gab and you have the proverbial talking head.

He is sure there is a correlation between the intuitive breakthroughs that have come to him in dentistry and the creative breakthroughs he has experienced as an actor-writer-director. Breakthroughs only come if you are open and available to them. It means preparing yourself for invention by putting in the work ahead of time and then letting your subconscious take over to incubate and birth ideas when they are ready to emerge.

"To me it is allowing your subconscious to think for you because your subconscious is always going," he said. "A lot of these discoveries in dentistry were being worked on just like anything else and then suddenly there it was in front of you."

He recalls the time the idea came to him of how a paper point used in root canals can be coated with calcium. "I always remember there it was right in front of me all along on the bracket table, and I had seen that a thousand times before, but now my subconscious had put two and two together, and I saw that putting the paper point plus the calcium together gave you a wonderful way of getting calcium where you need it—inside the tooth. I really think there are people who do not allow their subconscious to do much for them or they think, *If I don't think of something right now, I am never going to.* But the harder you try, the worse it is. That surrender to the subconscious—*I will think of it later*—is where those discoveries come from. And one kind of discovery leads to discoveries in other fields."

His life in theatre has not only served as an inspiration and gateway for his professional career, it has also served as a buffer and sanctuary from his life in dentistry. For Manhart, there is no greater satisfaction than knowing he has rendered service to patients. But the demands of dentistry, as with any profession, can be taxing. That is why he prizes having the theatre to go to. He can leave the work-a-day world behind in order to lose himself in a realm of make-believe.

"It is such a welcome distraction from dentistry because dentistry would drive any person crazy. The theatre is such a complete change that it's good for you. It is wonderful to go from the office and go do theatre, and completely forget you are a dentist and really use a lot of your talents and experiences to create something on stage," he said. "And for so many people, myself included, the theatre is where you discover talents and abilities you never dreamed you had. Theatre is so much a part of the world and you can learn so much from it. In other words, if you can play something on stage and you can do it in front of people and make them a part of what you are doing, you make people laugh and cry and solve their problems ... that is irreplaceable."

"The most fulfilling thing about my involvement in theatre," he said, "is that I get to show that the world *is* a stage and it is more rewarding to realize it in different ways than to be lost in a black hole of politics or religion."

As he says, the theatre can be a place to work things out, such as unresolved issues and emotions. It is a freeing space. Therapeutic even. Seen in that light, it is no accident he has gravitated to the therapeutic side of dentistry. You might say it is his calling. Reading, painting, listening to music, landscaping, dining out, and traveling are other pursuits that help him escape. Tennis used to do the same for him. Before that, as a youth, it was basketball. "Those kinds of things let your other mind work, free it up," is how he describes it.

His appreciation for the finer things extends to home. The residence he and Bonnie share is an open modern showplace whose many windows bathe the interior in natural light. Their passion for art and music is seen throughout the spacious, muted living quarters, including paintings he has done that hang on the walls and an upright piano in the dining room. They love to entertain, and their jazz nights transform their place into an intimate atmosphere.

Their love of nature and design is expressed in a walkout patio and garden whose landscaping Manhart conceived and executed. His knack for gardening comes from his mother and her proverbial "green thumb."

The serene yet dynamic living space is an aesthetic retreat that reflects the cultured couple who inhabit it. It is easy to see what drew them there.

"We looked for almost a decade for this home, stumbled on it, and bought it the next day in September of 2000," he said. "It and the three houses to our east were designed by

Stanley How, who must have been a serious student of Frank Lloyd Wright, the iconic architect of Fallingwater, the most famous residence in modern architecture. The design of our home, which was built in 1963, is nothing less than genius. Its modern layout is for all the senses and weather of this area of the world. The only things we did were move the laundry upstairs, put in some mirrors Wright would have liked and kept it simple and uncluttered. I hope to die in it. We have studied Wright's architecture a long time and have toured his buildings and homes, especially his Taliesin East and West homes. I see our home as an homage to his concrete, long-lasting contribution to American culture."

Then, too, there is the life we experience with our own siblings or kids. This is a bit more problematic where Manhart is concerned. He likes children. He fathered and helped raise eight of them, after all. But he has been by his own admission a somewhat distracted parent with a tendency to get caught up in his own activities to the diminution of his kids'. He can also be a bit of a distant curmudgeon who unconsciously withholds the affection and approval that presumably his children, even though they are all grown now with families and careers of their own, still crave from him, the strong, patrician-style patriarch. He also is not inclined to do family things or to attend family reunions unless persuaded or nudged, and then he invariably enjoys the gatherings.

Moreover, there is the life we carry on with friends, with neighbors, with associates, and so on. Manhart can hardly count the lives he has touched in the various guises he has filled, whether as doctor or teacher or speaker or director or friend or neighbor. His has been a long, varied life well-lived and one marked by all the connections he has made with people in his many roles. He likes the many hats he has worn and continues to wear. The fact there are many different constituencies and peer groups he can call his own is a manifestation of his diverse life.

Certainly, each of us leads an intense private existence that exists apart from but not entirely separate from our gainfully employed experience. A life of any length accrues with it a host of endeavors, roles, affiliations, associations, not to mention baggage, of both the personal and professional kind, whose whole is greater than the sum of the parts—each a reflection of different aspects of our self.

If nothing else, the biographical subject of this book, veteran dentist Mark Manhart, leads a rich life that seems a bundle of contradictions upon first glance. Now in his seventies, the native Omahan is equal parts old-fashioned practitioner, alternative dentist, "mad scientist," artist, pragmatist, dreamer, searcher, connoisseur, businessman, inventor, family man, lover, disciplinarian, libertarian, and iconoclast.

A contemporary of Manhart's, Father Jim Schwertley of Omaha, once told him, "Manhart, you are just like mercury, just when we think we have got a hold of you, you squirt out someplace else."

Manhart admits, "That is a fair assessment." Manhart's wife said, "I am going to put that (the mercury epitaph) on your tombstone." That is how "perfect" Bonnie thinks the metaphor is in capturing her mate's fluidity.

The word *mercury* comes from the quixotic Greek god of the same name. A derivation of that word is *mercurial.* One definition of mercurial reads: "being quick and changeable in character." That is not to suggest Manhart is a chameleon or that he acts a certain way one instant and another way the next, at least not anymore than the rest of us play various roles to suit the company or the occasion or the situation. No, it is just that he is one of those people who cannot be easily pinned down or pigeonholed because he is into so many things and seemingly all over the place at once. So, for the purposes of this bio, he might be dubbed Manhart the Mercurial. It not only has a nice, alliterative ring to it, it happens to accurately describe the man's multifarious nature.

All are expressions of his different sides and lives. But in truth there is no secret life for Manhart. His life is an open book, relatively. Isn't everything relative? His very public theatre work has certainly been no secret. His running for the Omaha City Council put him out there on the front lines of public-media scrutiny. His lay leadership in the Omaha Archdiocese made him a lightning rod for church-lay issues. His wholehearted embrace of the Montessori method of early childhood education put him at odds with the local education cabal. His attempts to introduce some of his calcium therapy innovations in the classroom met with stiff resistance and, eventually, resulted in his outright dismissal. His outspoken objection to traditional endodontic and periodontal approaches in favor of noninvasive calcium-based alternatives made him a pariah among dentistry's specialist community.

The person we become at seventy or seventy-five, if we live long enough to find out, is naturally an accumulation and a conglomeration of everything that has gone on before: the incidents, the milestones, the highs, the lows, the decisions, and the mistakes we made. Our lives are the product of many commissions and omissions. No one is without fault or blame. The best we can do, as Twelve-Step recovery programs phrase it, is to strive for progress, not perfection.

Manhart has something to say about this live-and-let-live ethos, too: "Long, long ago I decided to avoid reliving the past myself or through others, like raising the kids. If I had done one thing different, I would not be here talking about all this. All since would have changed, so history is what it is and regret is a cop out or a waste. I try to learn from the past, repeat the good parts. I love to read history and concentrate on the present, and maybe on tomorrow till about noon. I do not wake till 10 a.m., nor believe in God till after lunch. I try to see people from angles and steal the good sides."

2

Making Manhart: Hometown Touchstones

Born in 1937 to a large, traditional, devout Catholic family, Mark Manhart lived the first five years of his life at Thirty Third and Arbor near the streetcar line that fed into South Omaha. Not that many years before, the heart of the ethnic district known as South Omaha had been a separate city before the adjacent city of Omaha annexed it. For most of its life South Omaha was a working-class melting pot with large contingents of immigrant Poles, Czechs, Germans, and Irish but also Italian, Mexican, and African-American enclaves.

Today, South O is an immigrant's haven again, only the new immigrants are predominantly Latino and Sudanese. The big packing plants are long gone, as is the stockyards. But in their day, the plants and yards were meccas for migrants. The Big Four meatpackers, Swift, Cudahy, Armour, and Wilson, operated sprawling, multi-story brick butchering, processing, and canning plants that employed thousands of ethnic laborers. Feeding the tremendous volume of cattle and hogs required by these plants was the Omaha Stockyards, once the world's largest livestock market or exchange. The sprawling complex's malodorous aromas permeated the Manhart home and the surrounding neighborhood so thoroughly that Mark has never forgotten that stench.

The city owes much of its early growth to being well-situated on the Missouri River, to being a major rail center—it is headquarters for Union Pacific Railroad—and to being an agribusiness leader. Union Pacific's grand old Union Station is a sublime white stone art deco–style building that at its peak during World War II serviced ten thousand passengers a day, "That on very special occasions was a grand adventure for any Manhart kid to visit."

Manhart and his siblings counted it a very special occasion indeed when afforded the rare adventure of catching an outgoing train or greeting an incoming one. Decommissioned decades ago, the station has been preserved and restored as the Durham Museum, a Smithsonian affiliate that chronicles Omaha's, the region's, and the nation's past.

Omaha's central location and close proximity to cattle and hog stockers and feeders, combined with its world-class rail infrastructure, positioned the city to become a packing and

Manhart Family - Eleanor and Paul in the front row, center;
Mark is back row, far right.

livestock giant. Railroad, packing, and livestock jobs drew
many people to Omaha the first half of the twentieth century.

During the early boon times of the 1910s South Omaha was
called The Magic City. The acrid perfume emanating from
the slaughter houses, the rendering plants, the stockyard
pens, the livestock trucks that stacked up for blocks waiting
to unload their bellowing cargo, and the factory smokestacks
was called The Smell of Money. A host of bars, pool halls,
gambling joints, bordellos, boarding houses, hotels,
restaurants, hardware stores, and other businesses sprang up
to service the roughnecks and rowdies and working stiffs on
whose strong backs the city was built.

That blue-collar life was largely foreign to Manhart, who grew up in somewhat privileged conditions owing to his father's white-collar law practice. But, to be fair, Manhart's father and mother both had intimate acquaintance with physical labor, having each grown up on farms. And as a kid Manhart spent summers on his maternal grandparents' farm in Steinauer, Nebraska, where he gained an appreciation for working the land. But that does not change the fact he was basically a middle-class city boy. The family home, he recalls, was "near the streetcar, where we learned to put pennies on the tracks for the crime of defacing them."

His family had a local celebrity for a neighbor. "We lived next to Bill Myers, the director of the Omaha Community Sing, held each summer Sunday evening in the big parks all over town, from Fontenelle Park to Riverview Park (now the Henry Doorly Zoo), to the then-far-west Elmwood Park for the wealthy folks. He was great. His son 'Chinner' and I were best pals despite the fact I once tore a gob of hair out of his head for messing with a Manhart."

That was a time when disputes between kids were settled with some roughhousing, wrestling, pushing, shoving, or, at worst, fists, and not lethally with guns.

Mass singalongs were standard entertainment in the days before malls, megaplexes, television, computers, and text messaging. "Mobs of people came and Myers would lead us with his booming, melodic voice and bouncing ball on the screen (a sheet or an actual movie screen would be erected to project images)," Manhart said. "We learned so many lyrics of music that return today, like 'Harrigan,' 'Cowboy Joe,' and of course at the end, 'God Bless America.' It was the real karaoke for everyone."

When he lived on the south side of town, Manhart frequented a public green space that is part of an early Omaha parks and boulevards system whose grand scope and beauty were never fully realized but whose elegant vestiges remain.

"Hanscom Park on South Thirty-Second was our favorite with the pond for fish and ice skating, oak woods with trails, hills for snow sledding and racing halfway through the park on the handlebars of brother John's bike, balanced in back with newspapers for his route, and through the spray of flowers by Janousek's [a local florist]. Our Lady of Lourdes Catholic Church and school were across the street and just down Center Street was ice cream heaven at Reed's. What more could a kid ask for a playground?" he remembered.

When his father, Paul Manhart, traded homes with Uncle Pete, the family moved across town to Thirty-Second and Chicago in Omaha's solidly middle-class St. Cecilia Cathedral neighborhood just a mile or two northwest of downtown. The area is near the Gold Coast, a stretch of large, opulent estates built by some of Omaha's leading aristocrats of the late nineteenth and early twentieth centuries, include the Storz (brewery), Joslyn (printing), and Brandeis (department store) family empires. Their fortunes, if not literally made in gold, were substantial enough to inspire a name that connoted such wealth with streets paved in gold. These titans' business interests, leadership, and philanthropy injected vital capital, energy, and vision onto the Omaha landscape, not to mention they built some of the city's most distinctive brick-and-mortar edifices.

The Storz family alone accounted for several mansions and a distinctive brewery with its high smokestack. The Joslyns gave Omaha its only Scottish Baronial Castle and its renowned art deco fine art museum. The Brandeis family contributed distinctive mansions of their own but most memorably a downtown department store that dominated Omaha retail for generations and reigned as one of the largest, most opulent stores of its kind west of Chicago.

Even as a boy Manhart understood what it meant to move up in the world, and even though his family hardly lived in a mansion before or after the move, he knew that being surrounded by such well-to-do residents meant his family was on an upwardly mobile track. Moving was no small feat for a family that by then numbered ten kids. Two more soon joined the fold. The Manharts became a living incarnation of a popular book and movie of that era, *Cheaper by the Dozen,* that charted the comic misadventures of a big family. Hollywood remade the film a few years ago. About once a decade the industry revisits that old chestnut by making yet another idealized film about charming big family escapades. Reality is not nearly as romantic as those fictional portrayals, but has its own quirks, high jinks, and perks, according to Manhart.

"The family was a big addition to the neighborhood," Manhart said. "When older sisters were visited by boyfriends, they did not know what to think. Mary's future hubby, John Lomax, thought it was a rooming house or hotel."

A distinct advantage to having so many brothers and sisters is having a small army to watch your back. Bullies who picked on a Manhart soon discovered they had chosen the wrong family to tarry with. Fight one and you fought them all. "So it was like nobody messed around with the Manharts very much," he said, "because you would always have a big brother or big sister to send to beat up your tormentor."

Manhart soon found himself a new "gang" to run with in mid-town Omaha. "Upon moving to Chicago Street, I lost a few friends and gained far more. I ran with many fellows who had far less than we did, and then some with far more. Healey was always a great pal, rich in personality and determination. Mike [Healey], Phil Gradoville, Terry Finney, Tom Lee, John Fogarty, Dick McVaney, and I were life-long pals, half from St. Cecilia's and half from Prep [Omaha Creighton Preparatory School where Manhart still attended high school]. At Thirty Third and Cass Jimmy Hill introduced me to Gifford Park."

In that simpler time kids could roam freely without the stranger-danger worries of today. Neighborhoods were by-and-large adventurous yet safe environs to wander and explore. A watchful, tight-knit community of extended family, neighbors, school, and church kept kids safe and in line. Ah, church. For this oh-so-Catholic clan St. Cecilia Cathedral, which is the home of the Omaha Archdiocese, represented church writ-large. It was then and is now the place where priests in the Archdiocese are ordained and where other high masses are celebrated. Constructed over a period of several years in the early twentieth century, the Spanish Renaissance cathedral designed by Nebraska's preeminent architect of the era, Thomas Rogers Kimball, is arguably the most magnificent place of worship in the state. In keeping with the tradition of cathedrals, it is also a community resource that hosts many gatherings, talks, concerts, and arts events under the Cathedral Arts Project banner. Bonnie attends a jazz instructors' workshop there each March.

St. Cecilia is also a parish with a school. The Manharts were dyed-in-the-wool Catholics and that meant the kids attended their parish school—despite the tuition it cost and the extra mile or so it may have entailed getting there. That is not to mention the strict dress code, heavy religious education, and harsh discipline enforced at parochial school, where corporal punishment still ruled.

Catholic school taught by nuns in habits and mass said in Latin by priests in cassocks were fixtures in Manhart's childhood. Today, he looks back on all that with the jaundiced eye of a fallen-away Catholic who long ago became soured on organized religion. His lapsed Catholic status has been a bone of contention and a source of consternation with some in his family. Religion and politics are two volatile subjects he has much to say about, but he must often bite his tongue around family and friends so as not to start an argument that turns into a feud.

With his best as-through-a-child's-eyes recollection, he reconstructs the Monday through Friday route he took to get to Catholic school. Manhart being Manhart, he cannot resist a jibe or two at the whole business: "Yates public school was right across Chicago Street from our house for education, but oh no, we all had to walk a mile a day up the Cass–California Street hill with lunch bags to St. Cecilia's Cathedral Grade School. We usually took a pit stop at 36th Street just before the California ascent at Ryans', the next huge family 'hotel.' The mile down was best by Cass Street on anything with wheels. Not so much traffic to contend with. It went all the way down to Thirty-Fifth, and you could roll into home plate on Gifford's softball field, almost at Thirty-Third, safe and only a little shaken. That was critical to survival because I soon learned that some Dominican nuns and some priests had taken their final degrees from the Holy Roman University of Spanish Inquisition."

Besides the hard conservative line Manhart was indoctrinated in at school, he was reared on Depression-era values of thrift and community and on Midwestern values of industriousness and humility. He grew up neither rich nor poor but middle class. Of course, being one of twelve kids meant a certain every-man-for-himself reality. The worst of the Depression was over by the time he entered the picture, but it was not as if frugality was a foreign concept in a home with that many mouths to feed.

Manhart explained the way it was: "I cannot say I felt in a Depression because there were already limits to everything: food, room, clothes, goodies, opinions, travel, use of things like the phone, the bathroom, the car, your time, other people's time, and thousands more. It was obvious there were many kids that had more things than we did. You got what you thought you deserved."

It was also wartime. He pretended to stay abreast of the latest developments via movie newsreels at the theater and radio broadcasts at home that, along with newspaper and magazine stories, reported from the Pacific, North African, and European fronts on American-Allied progress against the Axis forces. War bond campaigns, scrap metal drives, and rationing of gasoline, rubber, butter, milk, and other products were regular home-front reminders of the war being fought far away.

None of his brothers served in the Second World War, but brother David Manhart saw action with an Army artillery unit in the Korean War, "and to this second," Manhart notes, "has said virtually nothing of it. Neither could I."

Faced with a scarcity of resources, said Manhart, "You always had to compete and be persistent." That survival-of-the-fittest training can steel one for the rough patches ahead. Manhart has had more than his share and yet he is still fighting the good fight. He comes from the kind of hardy stock that does not easily break. The Manharts endure. His father lived till age eighty-five. His mother until one hundred and four.

"Mother and Dad surely lived through the Depression and yet rarely came off as 'in crisis.' The impact was powerful—almost adulthood by age fourteen, about the time I got into carrying newspapers and going to high school."

Sweet nostalgia. "We all had a used bike early on. That and a yoyo. You had to in order to be anyone." He held that most American of boyhood jobs—a paper route, inheriting one at Station H, Route Fifty-Four. "It was the largest with the smallest area to cover, around the Mutual of Omaha building. I delivered to a lot of large old homes that had been turned into apartments. I met all sorts of people, mostly young women, collecting for the paper at their doors, asking for payment, in their casuals, at supper time, even in their smalls, up close." He has written a play inspired by his newspaper-slinging adventures entitled *54H*.

At home there was no doubting who ran the ship. "We knew Mother and Dad were the heart of the family, and that ain't just twittering," said Manhart with a glint at the all-the-rage social media phenomenon, Twitter, a digital medium for the gossip and bantering that used to occur between clotheslines and over fences, on porches, and at dining tables. His folks made "quite a tall handsome couple" and together formed quite a duo. Each came from a long line of doers. Just

45

like their folks before them, the couple persevered to make a better life for themselves and their children.

"I came from a family where either you helped out with every different kind of thing in the house and you ate food that was healthy and at the time to eat it and you slept at the right time, or you were punished—you did not get any food. Some way or another you were told that this was not appropriate human activity, to be running around the kitchen while you are eating or something. To be running around the house is simply not acceptable because this is not a playground. I was raised with that pretty rigid kind of education," he said.

He grew up in a rigid religious tradition as well. Several members of his extended family on his mother's side entered the religious life as priests or nuns. Two of Mark's own siblings took the vows.

The religious life tends to be all-consuming, leaving precious little time for family. That is why when his siblings entered that life it was a bit like losing them, especially his brother Paul. Clare remained more accessible, however. "We saw little of them other than their rites of passage in their orders. Clare is yet one of the closest siblings I have and she helped me choose not to be a priest, though she would not like to hear that."

For devout Catholic parents the prospect of a son or daughter taking vows is an honor and blessing bestowed upon the family. With two older siblings already dedicating their lives in the service of God, it is hardly surprising that Manhart, who dutifully served as an altar boy, considered a religious vocation himself. In the days when the priesthood was still unsullied by pedophilia scandals and by clerics shedding the collar to marry, the calling was an almost universally respected life choice. Far more Catholic boys considered the calling in that era than do today. Manhart was not immune from the prospect.

"When I got into high school under the Jesuits [at Prep], several priests thought I was a great candidate [for the priesthood], so it became a big part of my thinking to do that. And then, as I always say, I sat down and I let the feeling go away. It is kind of like this—I had a brother that was a Jesuit, ergo I am going to heaven, because that is a given right there, and so I did not have to worry about that," he said with his characteristic sarcasm.

Manhart's father, meanwhile, remained a hands-off Catholic who felt uneasy with the church's hierarchical structure. It was an attitude that presaged Manhart's own later healthy skepticism. "Dad was never what you might say captured by it (the pomp, the dogma, the bowing and scraping acquiescence). He was always astute, not above it, still a very loyal Catholic, but on his own—like he did not go to meetings much."

That kind of independent thinking is exactly what led Manhart to wean himself from the church and the powerful hold it had on him. "Growing up in a strict Catholic environment was hell on wheels, fueled by guilt and fear, two deep, difficult cancerous conditions for anyone to overcome and control. Most do not succeed. I still am under self-therapy. My family was, and some still are, part of it. However, without their caring I would long ago have been dead. Escaping the environment was incredible. Sunday Mass attendance with your family was compulsory, many times daily Mass. The ultimate values were to think over what you did since your last confab (confession), what to do till the next, and meet people. Talk about a gorilla off the back. Now I can do these anytime I want, anywhere."

Being Catholic in the pre-Vatican II world, before contraception became a somewhat acceptable family planning measure, invariably resulted in big families. The Manharts, while certainly not the norm numbering fourteen, were not as uncommon as you might think. Vying for attention and carving out an individual identity within such a large clan poses problems. Manhart's rather nebulous place by virtue of being far down the ranks was evident right from birth. "I come from a family of twelve kids. I was the tenth, and so when I came, my birth certificate just read, 'Manhart, male.' That is all it said."

He discovered his nondescript introduction to the world when he needed to produce a copy of his birth certificate in order to get married the first time. He figured his parents had enough on their plate with nine kids in tow by then, so that by the time he came around choosing a proper name for him right away was low on their priority list. "They were so tired from having kids," he surmised.

Manhart describes growing up in a mega-family as something akin to being an entry-level employee in a corporation. "Big families are wonderful but they can be really cruel. Well, all families can be really cruel. But I always felt like by being in kind of the middle of the family I was hiding out in a sense. There were six boys and six girls in my immediate family and, you know, the oldest is always the greatest, the youngest is always the greatest, and the rest of us in between were just left alone. I seemed to have had kind of a protected life on the inside of a huge family. In our big family we tended to be so independent we kind of, I guess, got tired of each other. As a result, today, we do not do all this family reunion stuff. We used to go to Mother's Steinauer family reunion every five years, and now it is the Manhart family reunion we go to every five years."

Because the Manhart brood was so spread out in age, twenty years separating the oldest and youngest siblings, there naturally were gaps in affection and attention. "My sister Jane died when she was about forty. Because I was much younger than she, I was never real close to her," said Manhart. "But as I look at myself, I was very much like her. She was artistic. She married a dentist."

How did Manhart get started on the path to being a dentist? "I remember at about fourteen years of age I decided to be a dentist. People say, 'Well, how did you know that would be the best choice? You were only fourteen, you were only a kid.' Well, I want to tell you, fourteen in my day was much different than being fourteen now, and in my father's day fourteen was much different than what it was when I was that age. At fourteen you were treated almost like an adult. I remember the old story—one of my older relatives was sent to this country and came up the Missouri on a river boat and got off at St. Joe [St. Joseph, Mo.], and a day or two later somebody picked him up. He was fourteen years old. I mean, God, that would be unheard of today."

It turns out there were some family role models who helped influence Manhart's decision. "I had two uncles and a brother-in-law who were dentists. They say a lot of it is in your genes anyway, and I believe this—that you have a natural talent with your hands and eyes. Some people cannot see three-dimensionally, and if you cannot see three-dimensionally, there are a lot of things you cannot get into."

Aside from the acute vision and dexterity required, he feels the right kind of demeanor is necessary as well. "You have to have the temperament to be a dentist and in a sense I had that." His ability to empathize and communicate with people, along with the confidence he projects, make him a natural with patients. He can be the authority figure but still be sensitive to patients' anxieties and responsive to their concerns and questions.

Those paternal uncles of his who were dentists may have had successful practices, but they were less than encouraging to

Manhart about his decision to study dentistry. "I really looked up to them until I got accepted into dental school, and then I wrote them about it and I did not get so much as a peep of an answer, and I just thought, *Well, I guess it's something I have got to do myself if I want to do it.*" He did, too.

Every path to dentistry is not the same. Manhart recalls asking a colleague once, "Why did you ever become a dentist?" He said the man replied, "Well, my mother took me up to the school and said to the president, 'What do you need?,' and the school president said, 'Well, we could use a few dentists, and she said, 'Here's a dentist.' He became a very popular dentist around here, too." Whatever it takes. All roads lead to the tooth fairy.

When Manhart did get accepted to dental school, he went to his father looking for paternal blessing and assurance he had made the right decision. "I said to him, 'Do you think I can make a living at this?' He said, 'Listen, there's always room for a good lawyer, so I think there's always room for a good dentist.' And that's the truth."

The Jesuit-run Creighton Prep was an apt primer for Manhart's later studies at Creighton University, a prestigious Jesuit institution of higher learning. Prep has always been a feeder school for Creighton, especially during Manhart's tenure there, when the high school was located on the university's downtown campus.

Then, as now, Prep was known as a private liberal arts school with high academic standards and dominating athletic teams. Virtually all of its graduates go on to college and most enter some profession. All of Manhart's older brothers, with the exception of John, had preceded him at Prep. As it was the "expected" thing to do, Mark continued the family line there. That same expectation sent the Manhart girls to then-St. Mary's, now known as Mercy High School.

By the time they reached their teens the Manhart siblings were responsible for paying much of their own way through school, an expensive proposition then or now when talking about somewhat exclusive private institutions. "You had to work to pay a lot of that if not all of it, or you did not go, and Dad was always a stickler about that," Manhart said.

St. Cecilia's parish had its own secondary school, Cathedral High, and when Manhart and some chums announced they would not be attending Cathedral but rather Prep, it caused a stir. Why? Two of Cathedral's best basketball players included Manhart and Phil Gradoville, and the way Cathedral boosters saw it, the two boys were abandoning the working-class parish school for elite Prep. It is an old story. Prep has always seemed to attract the cream of the crop. Accusations of recruiting student-athletes have been alleged over the years. From the vantage point of schools who lose student-athletes to the Preps of the world, it feels like a raid or a violation. The student-athletes themselves are viewed as traitors or opportunists by their old school-parish. Thus, Manhart and his buddy Gradoville were branded this way by some at Cathedral. It would be the start of a pattern in Manhart's life of his taking unpopular or controversial actions and stands and then defiantly sticking to his guns in the face of acrimony.

"There were four of us in our eighth-grade class that had decided we wanted to go to Creighton Prep. A bad thing to let out. The administration of the parish was not too happy about it because, of the four of us, two were very good basketball players. Phil Gradoville was really a great player and I was pretty good. So when we took our talent with us to Prep and away from Cathedral High School, while it was not quite a sin ... let's just say the monsignor was not too happy about us going."

The saving grace was that the schools did not compete against each other on the court because their teams were assigned different classifications. That spared Manhart and Gradoville the cruelest taunts and jeers that surely would have baited them if Cathedral and Prep had faced each other.

Manhart's high school graduating class (1955) was one of the last at the original Prep site on the Creighton campus, the same campus he ended up attending for his undergraduate and dental studies. Despite the upset feelings over his going over to Prep caused, Manhart remained on good terms with his old Cathedral classmates. "I have a closer relationship with those people I was at Cathedral with than I do with my classmates at Prep. It was such a compliment to me that at the thirty-five-year reunion of our Cathedral eighth-grade class, the big celebration was going on a trip to Hawaii, and they asked me to go with them. So my wife and I went to Hawaii with the Cathedral people. That's how close it was and I always thought that was wonderful. I really enjoy going to some reunions still. We went to our fiftieth graduation (reunion) from Prep and it was simply delightful."

His experiences at Creighton Prep and at Creighton University exposed him to a regimen or discipline of Jesuit education that undoubtedly helped shape the person he is today. He may no longer have use for the religious formation or indoctrination that is part of the Jesuit tradition, but he certainly benefited from the Jesuit focus on the humanities, active student involvement in the learning process, and emphasis on the "magis" (seeking to better) and the "metanoia" (conversion of the heart to God). The Jesuit model is all about preparing leaders for tomorrow and delivering academic excellence through the formation of the whole person, intellectually, emotionally, socially, morally, and spiritually. He certainly cannot quibble or have qualms with being a well-adjusted, well-educated, moral, spiritual, socially conscious man.

Whatever allegiance he felt to Creighton University was damaged when years later he was unceremoniously relieved of a teaching post there. "I have no interest in remembering, it is too embarrassing for the university," he said. With some prodding, he described the events that led to those ties being severed, but his account will have to wait for later in this story.

Part of his prickly nature is letting even the smallest slights bother him or reading conspiracy or mendacity or dark motivation into the most isolated incidents. He can get into black moods by letting his mind race or obsess over some insult he is sure was intentional. For years it used to nag at him that his parents did not take more time to watch him play ball. His father was not involved in the children's lives in that way. The same with his mother.

"I think he must have come to one or two of my basketball games, and we even went to the state tournament, almost won the whole state, and still it was like Dad and Mother had their life as adults, and as young people we were to build are own and do it in a very adult, independent way," he said.

With the perspective of time and being a parent himself, he has come to understand this somewhat at-arms-length approach his parents took. It can look and feel like indifference to the child, but it is really promoting self-reliance.

"It did not seem like Mother or Dad ever intruded into our lives and what we were making of it, even though they were there. At first, you got this feeling that, 'Oh, boy, my folks are never there and everybody else's folks are there.' But, in truth, not everybody. And you think you might hold that against them but, oh no, I do not at all. I see how different that is now."

That same parenting model, not so much the opposite of spare-the-rod, spoil-the-child, but more akin to Montessori's let-the-child-be, let-the-child-grow mantra, is the one Manhart employed with his own children. Manhart's wife, Bonnie Gill, noted that while he was by all accounts a good father to his children, he is estranged from some of them today.

"He was close to them in their younger years I think but he has always been so community-minded that I do not think he was there very much as they got to be older. I often say to him, 'If you would talk to your kids the way you talk to me, you might have a totally different relationship. But all I hear you do is lecture them or talk about your projects. Kids need parents who want to know about their lives.'"

Heeding Bonnie's advice, he tries engaging his kids differently now. It is a work in progress. "He is certainly not family oriented. I'm the one who pushes that and he is very glad afterwards. We have family Sundays and he has told me, 'Thank you for doing this.' And so in that way I have been good for him," said Bonnie.

Still, it is a struggle for him to change his ways. "He does not like the way my family gets together and shares the same house. He likes his arms' distance. He told me one time he grew up one of twelve kids and had eight kids of his own and he reached a point where he decided he's just done with that. It helped me understand some. That I can get my arms around, that I can respect, because I never had all that chaos. I remember when we dated he used to tell me, 'You have such a quiet house,' because I only had two kids and they were grown by then."

But as Manhart himself can attest, being on the receiving end of this kind of "benign neglect" as you grow older can be hurtful. Even though he was only a serviceable role player for the Prep Junior Jays as the team's sixth man, he is still proud of what he was able to achieve in hoops and a part of him wishes his parents would have reveled more in his play. "My coaches said I had great hands on defense."

He remembers, "The funny story about playing basketball for Prep came when we played Tech [Omaha Technical High School]. Bob Boozer [a future All-American, Olympian, and NBA all-pro] played for Tech during those years and nobody could stop him. I always joke about it because I am so proud of it. Our coach would say, 'Manhart, I want you to go in and I want you to get Boozer's spot and stand in it. No matter what, just stay there because he cannot hit from anywhere else.' Well, it worked because we went to State and Tech did not.

"But when I would go out and get Boozer's spot, I mean, my God this big black guy would come at me and knock me anywhere he wanted to, but at least you could distract him. The most terrible thing you could do to Boozer was walk on his feet, which I would try to do. You know, just keep stepping on his toes. If you could distract enough, he would miss once in a while, and that was my famous job in basketball. I always wish I could meet him today and remind him that I was the innocent guy he used to knock around," he said.

From the perspective of Boozer and other African-American players of that era, things were not so innocent.

They will tell you about the racial slurs hurled at them before, during, and after games and the veritable muggings they endured on the court and the corresponding blind eye that referees turned, giving less talented white teams a free hand to rough-house and talk trash without having fouls whistled against them while the slightest bump or look or comment from a black player would elicit an infraction, sometimes a technical, and even outright ejection. Boozer and his black peers recall games being stolen right from under their noses in these wars before packed houses of hostile, predominantly white fans and officials, at the Nebraska Coliseum, affectionately known as The Old Barn, in Lincoln.

Manhart marvels at how the game has changed from the rather soft, plodding style played in his youth to the bruising, acrobatic, fluid dance-above-the-rim it has evolved into today. "Well, back in those days I do not think basketball was as physical a game as it is now. Nowadays basketball is just rougher than hell. You just really get beat up, and it's due to the fact they do so much more. My favorite team was always the Boston Celtics. How wonderful they played. But today's players do things the body cannot do, but they do it. It's like ballet."

When he says it is like ballet, by the way, it is not merely figurative or hypothetical conjecture. Believe it or not, he did ballet. In middle age no less. That's right, he did the barre. He did not go on point and he could never do the pirouette, but he actually practiced this most demanding dance regimen.

How many ex-jocks can say that? When his daughters were young, they took ballet lessons. When his curiosity and big mouth got the better of him, lo and behold, the lumbering giant found himself in tights amid a roomful of women and girls. He loved it though.

"I was president of the Academy of Ballet in Omaha, and I was kind of embarrassed into taking ballet for a couple years. I had wonderful teachers. The control of your body from ballet improves [your athletic ability]. I became a better tennis player and basketball player than I had ever been before," he said.

His willingness to even try ballet is in keeping with Manhart's seeker personality and his interest in far-ranging disciplines, including those he is well-versed in himself and those well outside his skill set and comfort zone. He recognizes and appreciates ability and professionalism when he sees it. It is why he respects the various sundry fields his siblings and children ended up in. He loves sampling the diversity of life and enjoys seeing and experiencing the different ways people find expression for their own interests, passions, talents, and ideas.

His first formal attempts at getting in touch with his creative side came in high school, where he discovered a way with words, a flair for painting, and an instinct for the dramatic. Of course, having an appreciation for the stage is one thing and getting up on stage to perform is quite another.

"I was terrified of being on stage in high school and college," he said. The one time he mustered enough courage to act on stage he played a G.I. in a high school production of *Stalag 17*, the acclaimed World War II prisoner-of-war satire that Billy Wilder adapted into a classic film.

That was Manhart's one and only theatre credit at the time. "It was great and fun ... but I was scared just to be on stage, let alone talk, which is the second most frightening thing you can do in your life after facing death." He should know. He has been on death's door more than once. He rekindled his burning desire to be involved in theatre more than a decade later and this time threw himself head first into the fire.

One of the things holding him back in those intervening years was the way theatre people, especially men in theatre, were regarded by the general public. "You were a sissy if you were in theatre. In other words you were gay if you were in theatre. That's what my family even informed me. A 'good Catholic family.' I am sure some of my relatives even think that today," he said.

As with all families, the Manharts have had their inevitable upsets and disputes and conflicts. "Well, you know, you fight here and there and all this stuff," is how Mark puts it. Of all his brothers, he has perhaps forged the closest relationship with John, who is a few years his senior. "I think it is because John and I were what you might call the most business-like people. He is now a retired very successful businessman." In 1966 John Manhart bought Nebraska Air Filter, which originated as Nebraska Coal Company. Mark recalls when his brother first contemplated acquiring the business.

"I had just gotten into practice in the Medical Arts Building downtown, and one day John came in and he was very, very, very serious, and he wanted to take a bank loan [for the purchase], and he did not know whether it was a smart idea to start his own business of cleaning air filters of all things. Well, when he explained to me what was going on, I just told him, 'John, what the heck, you would have a monopoly in this whole area here if you just got your business off the ground.' And he did and he became very successful."

Not everyone may agree Mark Manhart has a good head for business, but there is something to be said for a man who has built a thriving practice and a strong niche for alternative dentistry in the very town in which he was made an outsider. This holding fast and being true to himself is a motif for his life. He will hold his ground no matter what, come hell or high water, because he is a man of his word who has the power of his convictions to stand firm against the rising tide.

3

Roots

Manhart's large family is one of those "natural wonders" he always talks about. The family is so numerous and spread out that he once dated a gal who turned out to be a cousin. He had no idea at the time but found out before it was too late. He loves the fact his mother's clan, the Steinauers, can trace the family tree clear back to 1262 or thereabouts. That's right, the thirteenth century.

Generation begetting generation has been dutifully, painstakingly recorded and that genealogical chronicling still goes on today. He has an appreciation for the good stock he comes from in the way a farmer or a horseman does for the seed crop and soils and strains and crossbreedings that produce a successful biological-genealogical line that keeps on producing.

For the Steinaurs, it is nearly a millennium since the tracing began. "We are talking about family, and that is what I see as terribly important in any kind of a city or any kind of a lifestyle," Manhart said. "It's roots and where you come from."

His parents hailed from farm families: his German ancestry father, Paul, from western Iowa and his mother, the former Catherine Eleanor Steinauer, from Steinauer, a southeast Nebraska town near the Kansas-Missouri border. The town of Steinauer took its name from her sod-buster Swiss immigrant grandfather, Joseph Steinauer, who founded it with his two brothers. The Swiss-German–speaking Steinauer brothers came to America as part of a wave of Swiss emigrants escaping famine and poverty in the early to mid-nineteenth century. Once they got a foothold here as homesteaders, purchasing one hundred sixty acres each at a dollar twenty-five per acre, they sent for more family to come.

The tiny town the Steinauers established might as well have been a Swiss village on the Great Plains because the residents' native tongue and customs were predominant there for generations. When a Swiss film crew arrived in the mid-1990s for a documentary on how the town was settled by Swiss émigrés, the oldest residents still fluently spoke their mother language. The filmmaker, Karl Saurer, is from the same Swiss town, Einsiedeln, that the Steinauer brothers were from. It is quite a ride to get to through the Alps.

In 1983 Mark's mother, Eleanor, made her first trip to Europe, visiting the enclaves where the Steinauers still live in great numbers. Mark and Bonnie have visited the ancestral city Einsiedeln, near Zurich, three times. Steinauers from Switzerland have come for family reunions in the States, events that draw hundreds from near and far.

Manhart and his mother appear on camera in the well-produced documentary, and it is readily evident the admiration he has for his ancestors, who braved any number of challenges. They endured brutal weather, they tamed unbroken land, they dealt with Native Americans, they weathered droughts, failed crops, illness, and extreme isolation. They endured it all in making a life for themselves literally from scratch, in the vast barren spaces of the prairie. They came there when Nebraska was still a wide open territory. They chose to settle in Pawnee County, along Turkey Creek, in 1834 because the land was good and cheap and the water plentiful. Nothing was given to them.

Everything they had or made they did for themselves. Through many hardships, unending toil, and perhaps some divine providence, they ended up prospering.

Some years ago Mark and his mother wrote a brief history about Steinauer that is inscribed on a state historic marker a couple miles outside town.

"That namesake town of Steinauer was really important in my life," Manhart noted, "because we spent a lot of our summers on the farm in Steinauer. You grew up fast then, especially on a farm. I knew how to drive when I was like twelve or thirteen."

Lessons learned on the farm rounded out those learned in the classroom and in church. As a youth Manhart was expected to follow a rigid program of Catholicism at a time when adhering to the dictates of church and country were synonymous with being a good Christian and a good citizen. Yes, to be a person of faith and a patriot meant essentially the same thing in many households. The Steinauers splintered along religious lines around the time of Martin Luther's emergence, with one branch becoming Protestant and the other remaining Catholic. That division was reflected in the Steinauers who settled in Nebraska, as some were Protestants and others, like his mother, were Catholic. His family's deep immersion in the Catholic church meant he could hardly escape its influence.

"Mother was very involved with the church, and when my brother Paul became a Jesuit priest and my sister Clare a Mercy nun, that put her a lot into it," he said.

PAUL MANHART

The Manharts have been part of Omaha's success for generations now. The family got its start in Omaha when Mark's father, Paul, moved from the rural life to set up a law practice in the city. While Paul ultimately found success as a legal eagle, he began his working life on the family farm near Panama, Iowa. Then he got it in his head that a life in the law was his true calling. The kicker to the story is that instead of pursuing the law close to home or at least somewhere in the Midwest or even the West, he headed for the East Coast and Georgetown University in Washington, D.C. That's right, he shook the dust and wiped the manure off his boots for a fresh start in the nation's capital, where in short order he earned his sheepskin degree and passed the bar. It is a journey that is practically Lincolnesque in scope.

Then, or now, it is not the kind of career change you hear about every day—from the cornbelt to the Beltway, from the silo to the courtroom. "I mean, he was a good farmer, and some time, I do not know why, he ended up going to law school at Georgetown University in D.C., and came back here to practice and became a very good lawyer," Manhart said with the pride of a son who still admires his father's get-up-and-go initiative.

Papa Manhart found a specialization in law after some early floundering. "It is interesting. He went to school and was failing criminal law, and they told him, 'Manhart, you are going to have to pass criminal law if you want to get out of here.' Well, he did, and he got one of the highest grades ever given," reported Mark, who was handed down the story as a kind of parental proverb whose lesson or moral is that with hard work and applying one's self comes reward.

His father mainly practiced civil and marital law. Beyond that, Mark admits he does not know much about his father's law career. That was how it was then in families. Fathers were breadwinners who shared few insights about their work with the spouse or kids. "He did not spend a lot of time talking with us about his work. It was like it is important to him and it is important to the family, now you go make your own life and that will be important to you." Manhart was the same way when his kids were still at home.

The elder Manhart left his farm roots for a new career as an attorney only to return to the Midwest. A generation later his son Mark left home for Alaska of all places, courtesy the Air Force, to return a military veteran and a seasoned dentist. Each was capable of making a go of it away from home. Each possessed a marketable skill and profession that could be easily transferred to another locale. But, in the end, they opted to make their way in life in Omaha. Roots, once planted, can be hard to dislodge.

Besides an affinity for this neck of the woods and both being professional men, the father and son shared in common a strong work ethic and a passion bordering on compulsion for activity, for continuously applying themselves to something, anything deemed fruitful or productive.

As the patriarch Paul Manhart was the good provider never content just doing one thing. He certainly would not be caught dead sitting idle. A prevailing thought in the Manhart family was that idle hands do the devil's handiwork, so better to remain busy. Sound familiar? Like his old man, Mark Manhart has always felt compelled, out of guilt, out of duty, out of instinct, out of some restless, yearning spirit, to throw himself into many pursuits. Again, like his father before him, he is a man of eclectic interests who finds no contradiction in the fact he loves dentistry and the arts with equal fervor. Each fills and satisfies something in him that he does not feel whole without.

Paul Manhart was an inveterate tinkerer whose major breakthrough became standard lawn care equipment. Mark said his father helped engineer one of the first rotary powered lawnmowers with a Mr. Iversen, a friend and business partner from Iowa, just east of Council Bluffs, a blue-collar town directly across the Missouri River from Omaha.

"They developed the first power lawnmower—gas and electric," declared Manhart. "I do not know how that relationship started, but after they invented the lawnmower, they went in business together in the late 1940s as the Rotary Mower Company. They assembled the mowers, and these things were selling all over the world eventually. When I was a kid, I helped with crating, but doing the drilling, putting them together that was above me, I was not old enough. My older brothers John, Hugh, and David helped build them. The power lawnmower was first put together in the tool shed of Iversen's place near Highway Six east of Council Bluffs, and then moved to our family home's basement and garage on Chicago Street [in Omaha]."

The story did not end happily though when the invention was effectively picked up and patented before Old Man Manhart could protect it. The fortune that accrued to the patent-holder might have been the Manharts, if only ...

If there is a lesson in this, it is that being an attorney and inventor does not necessarily include being a good businessman. As Mark found out, being a dentist and inventor does not necessarily add up to business savvy either, although he learned a lesson from his father's decision not to protect his work. As you will see later, however, even a patent is not a smart business move. No, success in one field does not guarantee or predict success in another. One cannot be a virtuoso in everything, after all. But the Manharts do help themselves. As they see it, the world is their oyster, and they want to open it up and experience everything that is inside.

Manhart's father was a classic combination of brawn and brains, and so when not being a lawnmower maker, he was writing legal briefs and actively working behind the scenes in local Democratic political circles. He twice sought elected positions—running for the Second District office in the Nebraska Legislature and for a seat on the Omaha District

Court bench. In yet another example of how Mark emulated his father, Mark made a run at an Omaha City Council seat and lost—his one and only stab at political office, although he has no shortage of opinions on politics and politicians.

The saying goes, "Behind every great man is a woman," and in the case of Paul Manhart, there was a formidable better half who gave as good as she got. "It is almost like this—if it were not for Mother, Dad would not have had a chance with a lot of things because she was so supportive. And how does it go? He knew how to say, 'Yes, dear,' and she knew how to say, 'Yes, dear,' back. This is a perfect example of how that worked. I was twenty-one years old before I even realized that Mother and Dad had eloped at ages twenty-eight and twenty-nine, respectively. She ran away from the family farm to get married in Omaha and got kicked out of the family for her trouble," he said.

Eleanor's parents disapproved of the marriage. An arranged marriage was still the practice in many families then. Eleanor balked at being told whom she was to marry. Besides, at twenty-eight she finally had met the man she wanted to make her husband, Paul Manhart, even if he was an outsider from the city. Paul did not back off either in the face of her family's resistance. The rift left Paul and Eleanor with a hard choice.

Mark said learning his parents' union had been forbidden and that they felt they had no other choice but to run off together in defiance of their families' wishes is an illustration of how sometimes "you find out things you do not want to know. That just blew my mind to discover that." In the end, he is glad he did find out. "That is important to me because that kind of happened to me [with Bonnie], and I always thought that was great. It was kind of like being on Nixon's enemies list."

Mark is the first to admit that both his first wife, Mary, and now Bonnie, have helped make possible whatever success he has had. Marriage is a partnership that only works to the extent that each partner is willing to invest in the relationship. Thus, he admires how his strong-willed parents wanted to be together so badly they risked expulsion from their families. The woman in such situations usually stands the most to lose but his mother stood up for herself and followed her head and her heart.

He likes telling the story of how his folks met and married after a whirlwind affair that pretty much skipped the courting phase. These were two people in a hurry to start a life together. "She was the queen of the family. Catherine Eleanor Steinauer. Dad was a shifty attorney who walked in the bank of Pawnee City, Nebraska (about ten miles from Steinauer) while campaigning for Second District representative, spied the feisty teller, and it was a first-sight romance. They wed at St. John's Catholic Church in Omaha and soon shared a little house at 43rd and Marcy Streets in Omaha." Manhart offspring followed on a regular basis the next two decades.

The couple were alienated from her family's affections despite the fact she married a fellow Catholic and despite the fact the two raised their children in the faith, from baptism to first communion and on through confirmation. By the time two of the couple's children embarked on religious lives, acceptance was forthcoming from her family. But that healing only came with time. When it was all still fresh, the couple's brazen move to elope put them on the outs, especially with the Steinauers, who quickly disowned the disobedient lovers.

"Mother and Dad were written out of her family, literally. As in will. It was a revelation to me because they started completely new virtually and ended up with what you have to call a very successful family, although it does not seem now to be terribly dramatic and romantic. It was a very successful life they created. Mother never allowed us to speak ill of the Steinauers. If she even heard us thinking about it we were in big trouble. We did not talk much about the Manharts either because Dad was always really rather reticent about that. He never pushed his family on us," Mark said.

Making it all the more confusing for Mark was the fact he felt torn between two sides of the Steinauer clan. Going back centuries to their Swiss homeland, a schism developed in the family that resulted in a Catholic Steinauer line and a Protestant Steinauer line. Both immigrated to Nebraska. Personality-wise, the two lines were as different as night and day, at least in Manhart's eyes, with the Protestants an easygoing lot and the Catholics much more uptight. His mother belonged to the repressed Catholic strain.

Religious and temperamental differences produced tensions that linger clear up to the present day. Mark greatly enjoyed the boisterous, fun-loving Protestant Steinauers, which made it hard for him to reconcile the fact his lineage tied him to their polar opposites. "I grew up and I always wondered why the Protestant Steinauers were such neat guys," he said. "These hard workers would go out and get drunk and be out at five in the morning in the fields. They were always so much fun to be with. And the other side of the Steinauers, my mother's Catholic side, were always pretty prudish."

In retrospect, Manhart interprets his mother's feelings of protectiveness for her estranged family as having instilled a lesson to let bygones be bygones and to not let past insults or conflicts rule your life. The moral of the story was to be your own person and to live your own life regardless of what others say or do and to not hold grudges, which can only hold yourself back. "There are more important things to do and to worry about than whether you got along with this person or that person or whether you are Protestant or Catholic or something. There's more important things to deal with. She was always that way, and that's not easy," he said.

His father was the same way, too, not much caring what others thought of him or what he did, whether it was the prudent thing to do to go against Eleanor's family or to give up farming for lawyering or to get his hands dirty with a newfangled machine like the power lawnmower. Manhart followed suit in becoming his own man, unrepentant in his own ways, undeterred by what others said or did that questioned him or caused him hurt. In later years Mark met several attorneys in Rotary who always spoke highly of his father.

CATHERINE ELEANOR STEINAUER MANHART

Growing up, she was known as Kitty. Later, she went by Eleanor. But as much as Mark is like his father, he feels he takes after his mother even more.

Her nickname, Kitty, Mark explained as an admiring son, came from the Old English term to describe an unrepentant lass. By the time she married, he pointed out, she was considered an Old Maid. But she was spirited and picky when it came to suitors or horseback riding or baseball or Model T car touring. She had her own mind about such things and was not going to let her mother or anyone else decide for her. "She was flippant. She did not let any of the guys catch her," he said.

When she still had not gotten hitched by her mid-twenties, "she was supposed to stay single and to take care of her folks in their old age. That was the tradition." But she had her own ideas, and when Paul Manhart breezed into town and swept her off her feet, she was more than willing to leave the family homestead in Steinauer and strike out on her own with him in Big Bad Omaha. "She was more quiet than Dad, but she was every bit as adventuresome, if not more. She was the one who left her family, and she was the one who went back to her family and pushed it right back in their faces."

Paul and Eleanor Manhart, circa 1980

Mark's grown to appreciate the fact that one of the shared characteristics that made his mother and father a good match was their avowed refusal to be anyone but themselves. Staying true to one's self, Mark learned from them, is a virtue to be nourished. It needs nourishing, too, because some people will not like you the way you are or because of the choices you make. It takes gumption to stand up for your own true self and feelings and to follow through no matter what.

He said his father, like his mother, would not be dissuaded in going forward with the marriage. Eleanor's family must have thought he had some nerve, Mark conjectures. From their point of view he was the big city attorney waltzing in like a carpetbagger to take what he wanted and leave. In reality, he was a more sophisticated fellow than they were used to. He had graduated college, after all, and had been in Washington D.C. He practiced big city law. That worldliness and confidence had to have been a threat to them just as it must have impressed Eleanor. He was his own man in the same way she was her own woman.

For someone as independent as Eleanor, it is no surprise then she was still living on her own at age eighty-nine. Her husband had long since passed and she was getting by. But as she neared ninety, Mark and other family members were observing that their beloved matriarch was beginning to slip. She was having increasing trouble managing on her own. Family were concerned that Eleanor was no longer eating right and that all that time she spent alone was not good for her. Even the simple act of getting up out of a chair was becoming a struggle. Mark's older sister Catherine Hogan lived a few doors down from Eleanor, and she and her six children saw that "Grandma Manhart" could no longer live alone.

Catherine convened a meeting of her siblings, including Mark, with whom she is close, and they discussed what to do. One option everyone agreed was not right for Eleanor was a nursing home. Eleanor had long made it clear she wanted no part of being placed in such a facility. Nor did she wish to be a burden on her family. In the end, the family decided the best solution was right before them. Eleanor was already spending much time at Catherine's home, where she enjoyed some meals and time with grandkids.

By this time Catherine was a single working mom. Her husband and the father of her children had left the family. The couple later divorced. To help make ends meet, she took various jobs with her brother John and, for a period of time, answered phones in her brother Mark's dental office. She and Mark and the other siblings figured that since Eleanor was comfortable at Catherine's and she had six children to help out, there should be enough support in place to tend to Grandma's needs for however long she had left. Besides, Mark and the rest of the family could easily visit Eleanor there. And so Eleanor moved in with Catherine and the kids.

Catherine had an automated lift chair installed to transport Eleanor up and down the stairs. Eleanor had an upstairs room to herself but she whiled away most of her days in the sun room on the main floor. Everyone figured that even with the change of scenery, a better diet, and more hands-on care and attention that Grandma would likely last only another year or two. To everyone's surprise and delight, however, she thrived being in the middle of a busy household filled with comings-and-goings, talk, and laughter. The activity energized her. Grandma and the Hogan kids bonded deeply as they made a new life together, discovering things about each other they did not know before. Mark and his other siblings also made a point of giving Catherine some relief from her everyday primary caregiver chores.

"We had it worked out where Mother was living with Catherine, and we would take turns going over to Catherine's to help, so she could get out and play bridge or go someplace or do something," he said.

Because the Manhart family is so large and so concentrated in Omaha, many immediate and extended family members visited Eleanor there and pitched in with her care as well. Grandkids, great-grandkids, nephews, nieces, sons, daughters, sons- and daughters-in-law. These interactions with Grandma provided a precious gift in experiences and memories the family will forever cherish.

As you might guess, Eleanor's health rebounded. She grew stronger, more vibrant. She lived a good quality of life right on up to the ripe old age of one hundred and four. None of it would have happened, the family is convinced, if loved ones had not intervened and provided the personal care that allowed her to stay at home. Grandma Manhart is an example of how personal, in-home caregiving can help seniors regain their health and retain their dignity.

4

Spirit of Invention

Like his father was, Mark is a free spirit, an independent thinker, and an inventor. After years of field tests Manhart patented in 1982 a dental material and method using calcium hydroxide compounds in a controlled state for specific therapies in the treatment of gingival and periodontal tissues of the mouth.

The use of calcium materials in dentistry is hardly new. But Manhart was among the first in this country to connect the dots by recognizing and demonstrating how specific compounds of these materials could promote healing in ways never imagined. The stage was set for Manhart gravitating to alternative treatments by what he learned from some early dentistry mentors and teachers. Dr. Donahue, one of his Creighton University dentistry professors, taught the use of zinc oxide packs as noninvasive treatments. At the time, Manhart considered the packs an outmoded and harsh approach.

It was while in his clinical years of dental school and after he entered the United States Air Force's Dental Corps that he was forced to perform invasive root canals (endodontics) and gum surgeries (periodontics) and witnessed the pain they caused patients. He promised himself he would never do root canals or gum treatments in private practice. He did avoid such procedures and began searching for more humane alternatives.

A *Scientific American* magazine article provided the first clue for what would become his decades-long investigation into calcium therapies. The article detailed how researchers' work with Rhesus monkeys showed that calcium could stimulate the healing of abscessed teeth or dead teeth.

Mark thought, "Well, we are cousins to Rhesus monkeys, so maybe I should try this on humans, because I just felt it might be a way that led to nonsurgical options. I learned in the service that you could do surgical root canals or nonsurgical root canals, and it seemed to me by just seeing that work that the surgical root canals did not work any better than the nonsurgicals and that is what the dental research was beginning to show. And so I took calcium materials that had been in dentistry since 1853 and found new applications for them."

In the abstract for his patent he wrote: "Calcium hydroxide has been extensively studied as a potentially valuable agent in controlling endodontic problems. However, the prior art teaches away from using calcium hydroxide in periodontal therapy ... the conventional experience is that calcium hydroxide pastes are too strong for the soft gingival or periodontal tissues. Accordingly, there is a need for a calcium hydroxide material which is formulated to control its strong alkaline properties so that it can be safely used on soft gingival and periodontal tissues.

"Along with the need for the dental material, there is a corresponding need for methods for using the calcium hydroxide paste for treating soft tissue, bacterial infections, and a variety of other dental complications. Nowhere in the dental literature or reference patents is there disclosed a comprehensive method of periodontal therapy using a controlled form of calcium hydroxide paste. The instant invention is directed toward these needs."

He has since discovered many uses for calcium and zinc-based materials in wide-ranging dental therapies and products. Some of the products, which he tests, mixes, and manufactures, have applications beyond treating dental problems. His Calcium Therapy Institute markets the products worldwide.

Product advances highlighted on the CTI website include these:

- The Calcium/Zinc or CZ Toothbrush
- The Calcium Carpule System
- Calcium/Zinc or CZ chips
- The Calcium/Zinc Home or Travel Kit
- The Oral-Cal Mouth Rinse
- Calotion Skin Lotion and Cream
- A calcium-coated razor for shaving

Here is how CTI touts some of its products on the website:

CZ Toothbrush carries its own antiseptic brushing agent for gum infection, teeth cleaning, bad breath, decay prevention, teeth whitening, and desensitizing. For the most natural refreshing cleaning, use the CZ Toothbrush anytime and anywhere, as often as you like, whatever you are doing. No sloppy toothpaste or rinsing. Give your mouth and teeth a mild Calcium Treatment in three to five minutes. The CZ Toothbrush will remain active for eight months to a year.

Calcium/Zinc Chips are for use in specific areas of gum infection and deeply pocketed areas between the teeth. The packet of CZ Chips is a several weeks' supply. The thin, small CZ Chips are placed between the teeth and slid under the gums (two or three per tooth). CZ Chips are more effective and safer than costly antibiotic chips, which have little more effect than brushing the teeth. Also, the CZ Chips last a lot longer and actively control infection, stimulate gum healing, reduce bleeding, whiten the teeth, remineralize the tooth structure, prevent decay as well as bad breath, and strengthen oral bone.

The Calcium Carpule System includes Carpules with Calcium/Zinc powder. They are easily adaptable to enable you to treat entire quadrants of teeth and gums right at home without interfering with other activities. These intense calcium materials are a more thorough, effective self-treatment. Just one thirty–forty minute session, with the Calcium Carpules saturated with Oral-Cal Rinse daily for a week, has the total effect of an in-office Calcium Treatment. This home care routine will reduce plaque, stains, bad breath, calculus, sensitivity, decay, and soothe the pain of canker sores or similar gum irritations. Furthermore, it whitens teeth and strengthens oral bone and makes your next dental visit a breeze.

The Calcium/Zinc Home or Travel Kit is a great self-care and travel kit. This is a handy home and travel aid during these busy days on the road. Traveling is tough on the nerves and the body, especially on the gums. The kit is a quick refreshing treatment of your mouth and skin. All the self-care materials are good for use at home or on any trip. Just one home or travel kit contains: The CZ Toothbrush, CZ Mouth Rinse (8 oz bottle), a disc of CZ Chips, and our newest product Calotion (Skin Lotion). The CZ Kit is effective for dental care and most skin problems.

Oral-Cal Mouth Rinse is an 8-ounce bottle of a Calcium/Zinc solution to clean and soothe the mouth tissues, to reduce bleeding of gums, and to desensitize teeth, as well as strengthen teeth, their ligaments, and the oral bone. Regular use of the Oral-Cal Mouth Rinse reduces plaque, stains, bad breath, calculus, sensitivity, decay and soothes canker sores or similar gum irritations. Furthermore, routine use of the CZ-Toothbrush with the CZ Mouth Rinse as a brushing agent, or with Calcium Carpules, whitens tooth structure.

Calotion (Skin Lotion) is an 8-ounce bottle for the protection and healing of the skin. It is easy to apply to any of the skin. The time-released formula penetrates rapidly and softens and protects the skin. Calotion is designed to treat many skin conditions without leaving an oily or smelly residue and also relieves the pain of burns and sunburn; reduces the blistering of burns; controls itching and infection of acne, pimples, rashes, and insect bites; softens rough and calloused skin; protects the skin before and after shaving; prevents leg cramps; reduces cuticle and hangnail formation; strengthens fingernails and toenails; soothes skin irritations and aches; controls dandruff and itchy scalp; relieves the pain and itching of wounds; reduces scarring from surgery or wounds; speeds up wound healing; revitalizes the skin or acts as a makeup base; reduces large pupura patches of the skin; and controls athlete's foot.

———————

Manhart is quick to credit others. He points out that his daughter Jane, an Omaha cosmologist/esthetician, helped develop some of the skin products and that his wife, Bonnie, helps devise marketing plans and presentations for the products as well as CTI website content. Bonnie is the one who prodded him to get on the Web fifteen years ago.

He justifiably guards his various discoveries as his proprietary intellectual property and capital. It is a sensitive subject for a man who believes his work has been hampered by strong opposition. His caution is further informed by the experience of his late inventor father, who chose not to patent his work and subsequently left the fruit of his ingenuity and labor to someone else.

"There are a lot of ways to protect your work," said Manhart. "We have patented, we have trademarked, we have protected them, yes, in a way that does not cost us tons of money and does not cause us any kind of legal problems dealing with them. In other words, enforcing this kind of patent is extremely difficult. The best way to protect your work is to keep working and keep making breakthroughs, like the dentist who designed a way to treat gum disease with baking soda and antibiotics in the '70s. From what I get out of everything, even speaking with the man, he has not advanced his method much further in this area, he has not patented, but he has become *the* expert in it, and a lot of dentists may not accept his methods because of what he did, but he did wonderful work. But he has not taken his work and opened the next door, and the next door."

Manhart is all about opening doors and walking through them to find the next big thing or at least the next best solution. Unlike many of his colleagues, he contends, he is unafraid where the doors may lead him.

"About every five years we come up with something just remarkably simple because we opened that first door. You get through the first door, and you find there are three more doors. In research or in science the best way to protect your work is to keep going and keep learning and keep discovering things before other people do. Get there the fastest with the mostest, like General Patton, that's the way you take Europe," said Manhart, a history buff who peppers his speech with references to famous figures and events from the past.

His disdain for the profit-driven commercialization and closed-minded attitudes of American dentistry led him to break away from the pack and to follow the beat of his own distant drummer, searching for treatment alternatives wherever he could find them, even abroad.

By and large, he said, "Dentistry in this country has become a marketing thing, it is not a practicing thing. It is for cosmetics, it is because everybody else has it," whether a crown or dentures or perfectly straight-white teeth. "It works like this, you are either a dentist who markets your dentistry or practices your dentistry. If you are marketing your dentistry you have one mindset; if you are practicing your dentistry you have an entirely different goal."

There have been times he has played the media card to direct criticism at elements of his profession and to provide the general public another point of view.

"In 1985 I told the media in this town [Omaha] that gum surgery was barbaric. That is a strong word. I have changed my mind. It is not barbaric, it is worse. In 1985 if you had gum surgery, you would lose more blood than if you had had abdominal surgery. Today, if you have gum surgery, you will lose more blood than if you have heart surgery. I have had heart surgery like this [he underwent open heart surgery], so I kind of know what it is and I have talked to enough physicians to know how it has improved since 1983 or 1985 or whenever. It has improved almost miraculously and that is because in medical science by and large medicine is allowed to improve all the time," he said.

Not so in dentistry he will tell anyone who listens. On his Calcium Institute website Manhart lays out in no uncertain terms his outrage at the exploitative way some avenues of dentistry are, in his opinion, shamelessly hawked and practiced in the United States. To the uninitiated his comments can read like a screed or rant, which they are to some extent. But they are also a genuine expression of how passionately he feels about these issues.

When Manhart has something to say, he is not one to hold back. He long ago stopped worrying about how his outbursts directed at the dental profession, whether written or verbal, may cast him in a negative light as a reactionary or a nut or someone with an ax to grind. He is less concerned with how he is viewed by his colleagues and more concerned with getting, as he sees it, vital information to patients that includes critiques of some traditional dental procedures and that promotes the alternative procedures available through his Institute.

"They are intended to be strong and the public has a right to know this information," he said of his often inflammatory comments. "What right do we have to conceal good dentistry from them?" What does it matter if some feathers are ruffled in the process is his rationale.

An example of a Manhart dig is when he goes off on dentists who are "practicing dentistry that just rapes people." New technology, he said, aids and abets dentists more attuned to gadgetry than healing.

"Lasers are nice and they are wonderful and everything, but let's face it, lasers kill tissue, and it is not like you can decide while you are using a laser what tissue is infected and what tissue is not infected, and what tissue is needed for healing and what tissue is not needed for healing. If you can decide that kind of thing with a laser in your hand going through someone's mouth, you are pretty godlike," he said derisively. "It is another of those approaches where the dentist determines he will decide what will heal and how it will heal and what is bad and what has to go, as opposed to doing something that allows the body to decide that. It is as simple as if you get a cut, put the tissue back together, put a Band-Aid over it and let the body decide what's going to happen. That is entirely different than using a laser."

Power toothbrushes are another evil in his eye. "It is very much of an overkill mentality with which those products were designed, and they were designed with input from dentists like me, I must admit, with the object of getting more people into the dental office. We were designing those things and supporting those things with the mentality of kill. Let's kill the bacteria and then they [patients] will maybe come in the office. The idea was, let's do something that will kind of exacerbate the issue. I can look back on that and say, well, we were right but we were pretty dumb, we were pretty arrogant."

He believes many dentists are over-reliant on X-rays and want to read more into them than is really there. "X-rays are no better than any other thing for diagnosing problems," he asserts. He also believes many dentists abdicate their responsibility by having the hygienist do most of the work for them. "So many people have come to me and said, 'I went to the dentist and the hygienist cleaned my teeth and the dentist came in and told me all I had to have done.' 'Did the doctor look in your mouth?' I ask. 'No,' they tell me. 'Did he examine the mouth, really?' 'No, the hygienist did.' 'OK, that's' nice, but she ain't supposed to do that, number one.' I just remember this lady saying something like, 'Well, he could have at least looked in my mouth.'"

He chalks up the anecdote as another example of how dentistry has moved away from the kind of common-sense practice he advocates and models. "That's right. This is old-fashioned dentistry and it is the best dentistry—open wide. There is nothing more important than experience as far as I am concerned. This high-tech crap, with digital, electronic measurement of the length of the tooth—aaaahh! Taking an X-ray and saying the tooth is so long—the chances of that tooth being so long, twenty-one millimeters, is pretty good. The average is twenty-one millimeters. But does it need a root canal at twenty-one millimeters or does the nerve come out the side of the tooth and on the X-ray it just looks like it needs a root canal at twenty-one? The chances are about fifty-fifty that it needs a root canal at nineteen or twenty," he said.

"You see, we are talking about millimeters, but in these instances it is very important. So depending on X-rays for diagnosing things and confirming things is only one out of three, four, five things to use, and that is really critical in what we are doing in root canal and periodontal work. Periodontists measure the [gum] pockets, and when you measure the pockets you do BUP, Bleeding Upon Pressure. That mentality is so terrible. It is like puncturing your skin with a certain amount of pressure to see when you bleed, and if you bleed at this point, it is diseased. It is so sophomoric. It has no place in dentistry, no place, and dentistry was told this at least thirty years ago, but we did not believe it," Manhart said.

The periodontal model is based on outmoded ideas, he goes on, "It is something we have grown up in, that we believe in, but when you look at it physically, clinically, outcome-wise you are totally missing the point when you say we believe this is infected, we believe that is a deep pocket and that tooth has to come out. Every other day you get somebody who calls or writes and says, 'I have to have all these teeth taken out, but they are not loose. Why does he want to take them out?' 'Well, in the X-ray they look terrible,' is the specialist's typical response."

But Manhart said instead of putting one's faith completely in what a subjective X-ray or BUP test may or may not indeed actually reveal, a dentist should do a more thorough, hands-on, deductive-reasoning examination. He said, "Once again, open wide, look at it, see if the tooth is healthy. I always remember it used to bother me that dentists were so closed-minded about this, and I realized they are working out of a religious belief. There is no other way to describe it, it is the religion of dentistry belief, as opposed to what we always used to call wet-fingered, real clinical dentistry. Whether it seems to work in the lab or in X-rays or whatever, that is not as authentic as the wet-fingered clinical dentistry with facts that follow facts."

Manhart said, "There is a big conflict in dentistry about outcome-based research versus evidence-based research." His calcium work, he said, is backed by both kinds of research." But, he adds, "If you do not believe the evidence-based or outcome-based research, then there is nowhere you can go from there. It is just like this group of dentists from Russia who contacted me about my work. They are doing it the way I did not tell them to do it. And there is nothing unusual about Russia, this could have happened in Chicago. These Russian dentists say, 'We tried it, and it does not work.' 'Well, how did you do it? Oh, I see, well, you did it wrong. Did you ever think of doing it correctly and see if it works?' I wrote this dentist in Russia saying, 'If this did not work on these patients, we have to have you report this very carefully and show that these materials did not work on your Russian patients. We have to publish that because that will be the first time in the history of doing this in over forty years that it did not work.'"

Again, Manhart does not mind being challenged. Indeed, he invites it, so sure is he that his results will be replicated and confirmed. But he cannot abide anyone rejecting his therapies without first trying to understand them. He simply asks that anyone utilizing his methods implement them correctly on a trial basis to see if they work or not, but not jump to conclusions based on faulty practice and results.

People go to the dentist for interventional or preventive or maintenance reasons. On the intervention side, it is either a pressing need, even an emergency, that cannot wait or it is an elective procedure that can be put off. The economic crisis that began in 2008 and that showed only faint signs of abating in late 2010 has caused people to delay nonessential dental work, which is having an impact on dentists who are in the business of aggressively marketing costly, add-on dental procedures that have more cosmetic than health benefits, Manhart said.

"Things are not going well for dentists all over the world because of this economy and that is not unusual except what is happened is, if your practice is based on selling dentistry to people who have a lot of money, selling them the idea of having dentistry, your practice is dying. You get that anecdotally from dental lab technicians because their work is dependent on that kind of dentist," he said.

"So when the labs say that our business has gone down the tubes that means dentists who have been selling dentistry are not successful doing it. Because people who had the discretionary money now do not have the money. Whereas, if your practice is based on need—that you need the work done because you are in pain, you have broken something—that is not discretionary, it is a let's-get-it healed-right-now need, and those kinds of practices are doing fine," he said. "And we see that every day. I could work seven days a week, we are so busy and that is the kind of practice we have been doing thirty to forty years. And that is the big majority of dentists, it really is, you just do not ever hear about them."

Manhart goes on, "The selling is not sustainable and it does not sell in small towns either. When you do your dentistry in small towns you are responsible the next day because you are the only game in town. The slightest thing that goes wrong you have to take care of it the next day; whereas in a big city you can get away with a lot more," he said, because there are so many dentists to choose from. If a patient is dissatisfied he or she will simply go elsewhere. There is nowhere for a small town dentist to hide. The ramifications of poor practices will bite a small town dentist in the ass and get him or her run out of town.

He said trends in dentistry make certain procedures all the rage. In the rush by dentists to perform the latest procedure and of patients to have it done, what is often lost in the equation is the efficacy of the procedure and whether or not it is indicated for a particular patient.

Because periodontal or gum disease is the leading degenerative dental condition, it gets inordinate attention within the dental community, and the standard treatments offered for it are where Manhart seriously breaks with many of his colleagues.

"Periodontal therapy came in like a Sherman Tank and kind of took over things," he explained. "It added a surgical, a very cynical word there, dimension to this romantic dentist who practiced like a doctor doing surgery. The mentality was, 'It must be better.' But before that, in the '20s, '30ss, '40ss, no one would do surgery because it was so terrible."

"But in later years then the specialist surgery for the gums was accepted," he said. "Well, that went completely against what we were doing, and in the meantime we had developed a nonsurgical treatment, and so you could not even talk in the same language or the same culture with the periodontist, and this has happened with specialists throughout dentistry.

When our profession started doing crowns, everybody needed a crown, then everybody needed a partial, then it went to surgery and everybody needed their wisdom teeth pulled, and the solution was every time something happens you take the tooth out."

"And then it became root canals," Manhart observed. "Before that, orthodontics. Everybody needed orthodontics and that is still the case in this country—75 percent of the children in this country get orthodontics, whether they need it or not. In other countries, 25 percent. You know why? Because the other countries accept the literature, that's very accurate, that out of any population in the world 23 to 26 percent of the population need orthodontic care and that's it. The government pays for it. It's called humane health care. Outside the U.S., if you want orthodontics just because you want it and your kid does not need it, you have to pay for it on your own. But in this country there are so many people who have the money and who want it for their kids that they get it."

He said "a lot of the remnants" of this dentistry-on-demand model "remain in the United States in all of those fields. When you get into the other countries where you have what you would call humane medical dental care, there are other people involved with the decision, not just the patient and the dentist. There are other people who are what you might call regulators—the government." He said in other countries stringent guidelines or conditions must be met before procedures such as root canals or gum surgeries are approved; whereas in America, he said, the prevailing attitude is, "you got the cash, you need it."

Manhart has little doubt many Americans are fed up with the high cost of dentistry and the exploitative way some dental offices and clinics operate. His sense of things is that where dentists used to be considered among the most trusted professionals and dentistry among the most trustworthy professions, aggressive, price-gouging tactics now have dentists seen in the same light as car dealers or ambulance-chasing lawyers.

In the case of gum disease, he flat out says no periodontal surgery is acceptable and has not been for decades with noninvasive treatments readily available. Yet, he said, periodontal surgery continues.

"When we went on the Web with our Calcium Therapy Institute site in 1995, the first thing we learned was there was a vast population—and I mean a vast population in the United States—who were dying for some kind of humane dental care in the area of periodontal care," Manhart said. "We got emails, letters, telephone calls from people about their terrible experiences. Real horror stories. You would start crying. We got so much response that we started to send our materials to people to treat themselves."

He said the rash way some dentistry is performed today is a travesty. In the haste to address problems with drastic, overkill procedures, he said, more harm than good is done.

He is suspicious of claims by dentists who say they will do some radical procedure and the patient will virtually never need dental work again.

"Well, I just wonder, because that is not what we see," he said. "I went to California and lectured to a small group, and out of nine patients who had severe periodontal problems every one of them had had either all their teeth crowned or most of their teeth crowned and the problem was not their care of their teeth—we dentists blame it on the patient most of the time—it was really they had had too much dentistry way too fast and they were way too young.

"When you get somebody not even forty and every tooth in their head virtually is crowned and they have severe periodontal disease, you have to sit back and say, wait a minute, what are we doing here?," he speculated, "because if you are going to do that kind of work on people, you better have a pretty strong guarantee that you are not going to have periodontal disease. Because if people have periodontal disease, then our work is what is causing it. If you have gum surgery and you are told that in three years this will have to be done again, that's failure."

Other kinds of dental surgery, such as grafts, are highly "uncomfortable and expensive," he contends, "and when you are finished you do not really have healing and nice gum tissue left, you have like scar tissue. It is really not healed gum, it's like putting a big blob of tissue on there and it looks like a blob of tissue indefinitely, even when it so-called 'succeeds.'

Does it make bone better and stronger and everything like that? No. Does better bone grow as a result? I have never read anything that says that. You have a lot of soft tissue, but are we growing bone underneath that? No. The principal reason is bone grows bone, bone grows soft tissue, but soft tissue does not grow bone. We have not gotten that far yet.

"With gum surgery, in every instance what you are doing is treating the symptom, you are not treating the cause," he said. "Why is the bone lost? Why is the tissue receding? You start solving the why, then you have got it, and that is what we do with the calcium. We solve the why, and it is not just with the calcium, it is the whole approach, like getting the bite straightened out. So there are good reasons for doing old-fashioned dentistry, very little at a time. You must be careful getting uppers and lowers together because if you screw up here, it affects the whole mouth," he said. "What we are doing is exactly the opposite from the radical approaches."

Trying to get his ideas across to dentists who advocate radical approaches, he has found, is like talking to a brick wall.

"Someone like that. if I told him what we are doing, would take what we are doing and manipulate it to fit them so they could make more money. I am sure that is what has happened in the past," he said, "because you are dealing with someone who has no way of thinking outside of that box. It is too threatening to do that. I could agree to disagree with them because all I have to do is keep doing what I am doing and I will make a decent living and then go to hell besides. I look at it this way: in learning these things about our work it was a struggle; you see it and you cannot believe it; and you try it and this is not the rule, this is breaking all the precedents I have been taught. That is a struggle. It is a worse struggle, a more terrible struggle, for one of these dentists to accept any of this."

5

Discovery

The arrogance of organized dentistry in this nation tends to discount or ignore research done in other countries and to only accept American research, in the world according to Mark Manhart. As a result, some best practices are lost to American dentists who do not take the time or make the effort to seek out new ways of doing things that may not be prescribed by the American Dental Association or American dental colleges.

Manhart scornfully calls the ADA and dental colleges "the gatekeepers." He does not think it is healthy for these organizations to pass judgment on and, thus, approve or reject what dental findings and techniques member dentists or teachers or students are provided under the ADA's or the colleges' auspices or blessings.

"I have been told, 'How dare you teach something that you did not learn from your school? How dare you do a procedure that has not been approved by the American Dental Association?' See the kind of resistance you are dealing with?" he posed rhetorically.

"The American Dental Association has no right or ability or legal process to tell any dentist what to do—how to practice, whether they should be given a license. It is not the responsibility of the American Dental Association to do any of that. They have taken that on as a pseudo role in order to do one thing: protect the dentist from the patient, and that is *the* role of the American Dental Association," Manhart said, "and the schools are abetting in that process, whether they like to admit it or not."

To Manhart, it is the height of arrogance and ignorance that instead of a free flow of ideas in organized dentistry, there is a punitive, arbitrary gatekeeping system. He long ago discarded the parochial view that everything he needed to know fell under the purview of organized dentistry. If anything, his experience of practicing dentistry in the Air Force exposed him to newer, faster, better, more pain-free ways of doing things by dentists from all over the country, which in turn prepared him to question the status quo and to search for answers wherever his inquiries took him.

Access to dental research and practices not approved by the ADA and by dental colleges is much easier to come by now in this digital information age than it was before, chiefly due to the proliferation of almost limitless data on the Web. Manhart is like a kid in a candy store every time he goes online because there is no gatekeeper curtailing his curious mind. The only limit on him is his own imagination and ingenuity and motivation. He can use the Internet to help answer questions or to find clues and guides to his own discoveries or to read about new advances or to find out about techniques, trials, trends, products, and on and on.

The more calcium studies he looked at from disparate, reputable sources, the more convinced he was that the substance held promise for far-reaching therapies. "I really began to look into research done in other countries and started picking up bits of research and probably the best and the first came from South America—Dr. Roberto Holland. And there were researchers from other countries, too. I would spend evenings in the library, back when you had to look it all up in the books themselves (rather than on the Internet), and you would get little pieces of research that would kind of confirm that suspicion," he said, that calcium offered a world of possible applications.

He steeped himself in the data. "Man, it was like I would get lost. I mean, I would literally get lost in what I was doing and things just happened that made me think you have to change your mind about these things. So I took these findings and studied them. I knew, for example, that calcium stimulated some healing inside the tooth. That was real common. Therefore, I just translated that to the rest of the tooth, clear up into the root and the end of the tooth, which amounts to a root canal."

The next hurdle was actually applying his theory in practice. He did for the first time in 1965. It took some nerve.

"I had a lady who had a draining abscess, a dead tooth, and I treated it. But I put the calcium right into the bone, right into the hole in the bone, where the abscess was. I said, 'Well, I better see her in three days because this could be harmful.' No one had ever really put that into a methodology before and so that is what I did. There are several different kinds of these calcium materials, and I just picked out the one that I thought would take the least chance. It usually takes quite a while for a draining abscess to heal in the mouth, and if you got it to heal in a week that was really good. Usually it was a couple weeks before you really got good healing," he observed.

What happened with the woman patient who served as his guinea pig was nothing less than remarkable. He could not believe his eyes.

"In three days she came back, and I looked in her mouth and everything was normal, so I thought, 'Well, I must have treated the abscess on the other side.' But it was not on the other side, nor was there a visible sign of an abscess on the side I had treated. You could not even find any indication that there had been an abscess present. Plus, the tooth had been perfectly comfortable for her and still was. All of that made me just put down my equipment and go into my office and cry. It was so profound to me. I sat down in my office and I cried. I said to myself, 'What the hell are you doing?'"

That experience and others like it led him to approach the head of the biology department and an organic chemist at the University of Nebraska at Omaha. He described to them what he was witnessing, and they offered insights into the biological-chemical processes at work that explained the results he was getting.

"I began to figure it out," he said. "We were talking about free calcium ion and free zinc ion and how effective and necessary they are for almost any cell in your body to function. These calcium materials control the growth or the replication of the bacteria and so they gradually die off."

He goes on, "We did a research project with the same organic chemist and a microbiologist that found that it took about ten hours to get the bacteria to die off. We found that if you apply that to the activity of a tooth when you treat it, you come up with about the same thing. It takes a half a day, a day, maybe two days, where you have a gentle control over that bacterial activity. Then when it gets that low, you try to keep it that low and then seal the tooth up, and then the body thinks, *I'm OK with that tooth, I think I will keep it.* The properties that are given off by these materials are ionic calcium, ionic zinc. Zinc is wonderful for soft tissue healing, any kind of soft tissue. The calcium is great, too, but it was able to penetrate that tooth structure so efficiently that it in a sense healed the tooth by mineralizing it and closing it off to the mouth. You could say heal the tooth, but not in the skin sense or in the sense of soft tissue, but in hardening it and making it more resistant to bacteria."

"So I got it down to a methodology," Manhart recalls. "In other words, no one had ever done that before, of saying this is step one, two, three, four to do a root canal with calcium materials themselves. I put that in what you might call a method, and there's so many steps in that, and that method has kind of evolved over all these years to where now we are doing it in what we think is its most efficient form."

It was a eureka moment that shook him to his core, "I published that. It took me a lot of years—seventeen to be exact. I always remember it because it took Benjamin Franklin seventeen years to convince the Royal Academy that there was such a thing as electricity." Having succeeded in developing effective applications for endodontic (diseases of the tooth pulp) care, he next turned his attention to calcium therapies for periodontic (diseases of the gum tissues) care.

"I figured out how to do that with root canal work, and in about a year or so I figured out how to use the same type of materials for gum/tooth problems and what are called trifurcation problems," he said. "A molar has three roots and there is a place in the middle of those roots called the trifurcation, and the basic rule was if the trifurcation was infected, the tooth is not going to make it and you have to take it out. That was very, very common. Well I found I could treat the trifurcation area on the outside of the tooth two, three, four times, save that tooth, and nothing else would have to be done. The gum outside healed and the tiny canals of the trifurcation calcified closed."

"I figured out years later why that occurs, and it also explains why a lot of what we are doing at the Calcium Therapy Institute now works," Manhart said. "It is basically because the calcium is sucked up by the structure of the tooth, and it hardens the tooth and makes the tooth itself resistant to decay and bacteria, and so the teeth heals. In no time I was using it on a lot of other things."

That calcium is important in the remineralization of teeth is a long accepted, long understood phenomenon. But what Manhart discovered is that by controlling the introduction of calcium through applications of concentrated calcium compounds, the remineralization process could be enhanced.

"The rate at which it remineralizes is really very rapid," he said. "If you put something on a tooth, it is going to work quickly, but it is going to use it all up, and it is ready for more, but then you are not there with more. But if you had something that you could put in the mouth and it stayed for hours and days at a time, the remineralization would be rapid, but it would be better that it have a long period of time. The source of the free calcium has to be available for more than just ten seconds."

He gives an example, "With things like fluoride, you apply it and it's there for half an hour. Well, that's pretty good. The Europeans figured that out by adding a resin, but it took twenty-five years to be accepted in this country because it was done on Europeans and not on U.S. citizens. A half hour, that is great for fluoride treatments.

"But we have a very safe material that you can put in the mouth where the calcium ion, this massive amount of calcium, is available for about five or six days. Well, that really gives it time. It not only gives the enamel time to remineralize deeply, but it whitens the teeth. For that fluoride ion to work, it needs the calcium ion. And so my question is, if the calcium remineralizes the tooth and you can do it for a long time, over days, and the fluoride ion does not work unless it has calcium ions and saliva, why do we need the fluoride? Really we don't," he theorized.

"The fluoride does remineralize the tooth, it makes the tooth more resistant to decay, but so does the calcium. And which one is better? I am not sure. I would like to see some research done on that. More research should have been done on what we are doing a long time ago," he said.

What about this process makes teeth resistant to decay?

"It simply hardens it," he said. "It is filling in all the little ionic spaces where the decay can begin." Resistance to decay translates to resistance to acid. "You have to have this combination of debris and saliva, which ends up to be acidic. The bacteria do not eat the tooth structure, but the acidic residue or toxins from bacteria are what weaken the enamel. Bacteria of the mouth cannot replicate as well in an alkaline environment.

"But, you see, that is even taking a very narrow view of what causes decay or causes gum disease—that it is something the bacteria cause. When you dehydrate the enamel, and that is what bleaching does, it sucks the calcium right out of it. That weakens the enamel rods, which are chucked with calcium, and the calcium ion is so small that it can just walk right in between those rods very easily. It penetrates. You can almost see it doing that when you use the calcium. In other words, we use the calcium every time we clean people's teeth, and you can see that your calcium paste layers stay on the tooth, it just hangs around, it stays on the gums because there is zinc in it and the gums love zinc. So you polish the teeth and they rinse their mouth and it kind of hangs around. You do not see that with the other kind of polishes. They rinse their mouth with those others and it is gone. But with the calcium, you can almost see it being absorbed by the tooth."

"And so if you put calcium under the gums," Manhart said, "it is breaking down slowly, very, very slowly over days, and then it is continually putting off, giving off its free calcium, and that is going all over the mouth."

The more Manhart worked with calcium materials, the more possibilities he discovered for their therapeutic benefits.

"It led immediately into treating the gums because that is what you are doing, you are putting this stuff under the gums and we have been doing that for many years. We

got into doing sections of the mouth for gum problems, and then the whole mouth. Within a year we were doing full mouth treatment, and then we learned how to not just apply the calcium but apply dressings that make it even more effective," he said.

"You could take somebody who had severe inflammation of the mouth, of the gums, and apply the calcium, put dressings over it, have them keep the dressings on there for three days, take the dressing off, and it would be like they had the most perfect surgery and it has all healed. By contrast, if you do the gum surgery, you have to keep the dressing on for twelve days for it to heal and it is agony—there is not a kinder word to say."

He said where it involves several steps for orally ingested calcium or calcium supplements to be absorbed by the body, his treatments act faster and more directly. "To get from your stomach out into your gums or teeth takes five or six completely separate biological transactions. It goes from the stomach into the stomach walls into the blood, around the body, into the blood, into the bone and after about five of these steps, it gets to the tissues you want it in. What we are doing is taking the free calcium and the free zinc in one step and it is on the tissues, on the tooth, it is there. That is much more efficient.

"What we have found using the calcium materials is that we cannot practice without it. I would not practice without it, and this is one reason: we know if we have got a problem tooth or a problem area, if we treat with calcium, it will heal virtually everything except inside of that tooth. Any problem that is really inside of that tooth the calcium cannot reach. It may feel a little better, but if you treat and you have the same kind of symptoms cropping up, then you know there is something wrong inside. And so this is why I call it a great diagnostic tool, because usually people come in and they say, 'It's all over this area,' meaning the soreness or sensitivity. You treat, everything gets better, except that one tooth," he explained.

"It is a wonderful diagnostic tool for gum disease, too, and this is one of the great secrets we discovered: put it into a [gum] pocket and if it does not bleed immediately for about ten seconds there is not enough infection there to worry about; if you put it under the gums and in that pocket and there is infection there, it will bleed immediately for about ten seconds. It stops bleeding, everything calms down, everything starts to heal. That is a wonderful diagnostic tool."

Arriving at that understanding, he said, was scary, "Talk about struggling, here we were, injecting this stuff under the gums and we get this huge bleeding. That is scary until you realize, give it a few more seconds, it stops and it works perfectly after that. You start asking yourself, why does it occur? I am not even exactly sure why it happens. It is a wonderful arena to investigate."

As Manhart found out the hard way, many dentists are predisposed to outright reject new methodologies advanced by someone like himself, who is not a specialist or a researcher per se and who certainly is at odds with organized dentistry and thus viewed as a fringe practitioner. "The struggle with that is that nobody would talk with me about it, in the sense that I would go to meetings and wanting to talk to people about this and I would get this glazed look that was like, 'This kid is insane.' Worse yet, I told this dentist, and he said, 'Well, what do you use?' and I told him calcium hydroxide, because that is the way we always used to refer to it, because that is basically what it is and is still called. But there are a lot of different forms of it.

"This dentist said, 'What else is in it besides calcium hydroxide?' And I told him, 'Well, there is an ester in it—a salicylic ester.' So he goes home and he takes aspirin, which is an acetyl-salicylic acid. Well, I had told him it was an ester, a salicylic ester. Esters are in everything, you know they are in the body, in food, in plants, it's so common it is almost like air. Esters are very noninvasive chemicals, usually. A cousin to that is salicylic acid. But this dentist heard acetyl-salicylic acid or aspirin, and so he put that in his patients' mouths," Manhart said.

"Well, the next time I saw him, he gave me all kinds of hell for harming his patients, and I don't blame him because I know if you put aspirin on a tooth, it hurts like hell, it really does, and on the gums it really burns. The trouble is he just did not listen.

So after that I really tried to avoid these quick explanations, which can lead to these unfortunate misunderstandings."

Calcium hydroxide is a red flag for dentists, which is why it was ill-advised for Manhart to use that term.

"I soon found out we have to stop saying that because when you say calcium hydroxide, it immediately conjures up a specific chemical that is really very alkaline and harsh," he said. "I found that when I said to dentists it has got calcium hydroxide in it, they would just immediately turn off. So I just started trying to be careful to say calcium and zinc, and actually that is more accurate than saying calcium hydroxide or zinc oxide. Those are combinations, but they are a lot different than the element itself alone, calcium alone, zinc alone, and that is like the working ion of the whole thing anyway. It is not the calcium hydroxide ion, it is the calcium ion that is the working agent."

Still, some dentists are prone to jump to the calcium hydroxide conclusion or assumption whenever calcium therapies are discussed.

The insights Manhart gained into calcium as a healing agent made him eager to share his findings with the dental world, only the dental world, at least as expressed in America, did not embrace his ideas.

"In 1982 my research came out in an article published in the world's leading dental journal, The Triple O, *Oral Surgery, Oral Medicine, Oral Pathology,* and there was a humongous positive response from general dentists from all over the world," he remembers. "Specialists though were very, very skeptical about the whole thing. The response from the endodontists, the specialists in that field, was really negative. I mean, it was so horrendously negative I had a hard time getting through that. There were anonymous phone calls, anonymous letters. A guy calls on the phone and gives me hell for doing this, and I knew who it was as soon as I heard his voice telling me that I was way out of bounds in promoting nonsurgical stuff, especially with calcium materials. That I did not have any right acting like I knew something about this.

"You see, this is a fundamental thing in dentistry and probably medicine too—that the general family dentist is considered the dumb one on the scale, and if you have a specialty you are the smart one."

It is just that kind of caste or class system that he feels holds back American dentistry, discouraging innovation and experimentation and the free exchange of ideas. When Manhart attempted to share his findings with colleagues and students at Creighton University, he was reprimanded and then let go.

"That is one of the reasons I lost my job," he said. "I wanted to teach these guys how to do root canals efficiently and I wanted to teach them three or four ways, each of which requires but a third of the time or a quarter of the time as the prescribed way. The answer to me was very cold—'They will learn one way and it is our way or get out.'"

That same kind of paternalistic stance and, some cases, virulent attacks soured him on the state dental conventions where he used to present. The Iowa Dental Convention was one of his favorites.

"I used to go there every year and they were very polite, smart, very nice, and then some specialists started getting their way and I was no longer invited. I got tired of quarreling with dentists, so I just decided I do not need to have this in my life and I quit going to any of them in this country." He said one well-placed dentist spoiled things for him in Iowa. "We have had dentists over in Iowa who have been badmouthing our calcium therapy root canal treatment ever since, and it is because of one specialist over there. He thinks he knows everything about calcium and he keeps missing the point. It is calcium, it is not calcium hydroxide. He has just infected his prodigy, the dentists of Iowa, with this kind of misinformation."

Manhart said that if any of these detractors and defamers would care to do so, they could search and find plenty of corroborative evidence or support for his calcium practices. For example, he said there are dentists in places "like South America who have done calcium and calcium hydroxide research so beautifully well that we use them as our first reference. Dr. Roberto Holland of Sao Paulo, Brazil, has trained that whole thinking at the university and in the city to take a much better view of the benefits of calcium or calcium hydroxide materials, and his own work confirms everything we have done. And in fact in recent years research came out of Turkey, which can not only confirm Dr. Holland's and our original work but those things we have discovered since, including a nasal palatine cyst treatment."

He is convinced that his advances merit more investigation and scrutiny and he is sure that had they long ago been more widely published and subjected to "the normal process of scientific trial and error, challenge and not challenge, we would have come up with a minimum of twenty wonderful research projects that would be wonderful for dentistry today. That is the only regret I have about this whole issue—that that normal process did not occur because rather than open, in-the-light-of-day challenges of my work, there have been insidious, under-the-table challenges.

"We have always hoped someone would come out in print and say, 'We do not believe this, we will take it and we will test it and first of all we will learn how to use it, and then we will test it and prove this does not work.' That is the way science should work. But in my case I know it was decided by one of these gentlemen agreement conspiracies, it's as simple as that. That they would not challenge us because they knew if they did they would have to admit that it works and that has been a great disservice to my profession. That is the biggest disservice to my profession." Manhart can only wonder what might have been had there been that point-counterpoint scientific inquiry and exchange.

NETWORKING ABROAD

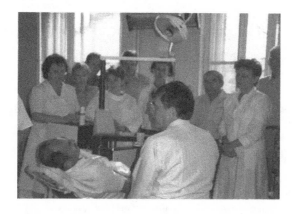

Mark sharing calcium methods with dentists in Poland

He chalks up this aversion to new ideas to the entrenched old guard or old boys' network as being resistant to change and defensive of their own turf. In stark contrast is the welcome reception his ideas get in other parts of the world. In a journal-like writing style, he recalled one of his and Bonnie's favorite sojourns, in Poland:

"Five weeks in Poland, 1991, just post–Berlin Wall coming down, and in several European countries. It was very special lecturing at Warsaw and Torun Universities to almost all female dentists who were twenty years ahead of my USA colleagues in science and twenty years behind us in high-tech equipment. It was terrific for putting global dentistry in perspective. What I sensed in '91 and what has been confirmed in a recent *New York Times* article is how USA science since Nixon has been intentionally kept in small, safe advances by the National Institutes of Health, research sponsors, universities, and everyone else so that no one suffers setting aside the horse and buggy for auto and airplane.

"The great science, especially dental, has been done in other countries where professionals are taught to think instead of sell, as I found in Spain when I went there in early 2009. It is consistent with how my research contract with the University of Nebraska at Omaha has been totally ignored and the review committee's comments will brook no response. That is the reality at work. Nothing risky, no breakthroughs, keep everyone safe while, as a patient wrote the other day, 'the patients suffer misery at the hands of dentists.' The public sensed this a few decades before, and now the news appears in the *New York Times*."

As has been his experience whenever he ventures outside the U.S. to propagate his calcium therapies, Manhart is greeted not with derision or suspicion or hostility but with interest. "Warsaw University called in students to hear the lectures," his written reminiscence continued. "Polish dental clinics may have had a few busy body bees or flies buzzing about, but the students knew about, listened intently to, and asked intelligent questions of our breakthroughs in calcium materials for dental therapies. My peers back in America are still grumbling, walking out, yelling obscenities, ignoring, or crying over calcium therapies today even as patients come from all over the country, from all over the world even, almost every week, to Omaha for calcium treatments."

Going to Poland or any foreign country on a dental mission always leaves time for more than just business. His travel diary recalled some adventures from the Poland trip:

"We wanted to buy china to bring home and so we went in a travel agent shop and asked for china. 'No, china, like in Polish, pocelana.' 'Oh, sure, no problem. You walk six blocks, tram stops. No problem, big porcelana, china. No problem, okay?' After trudging six blocks between each tram stop six times, stopping to ask about porcelana six times, even at the original castle of the Holy Roman Empire, and spying a bright poster that Chopin was to perform that night down the street, we called our guide Bogdan and asked he pick us up on a corner without shops, just a gigantic building with armed guards pacing to and fro. Shortly, Bogdan dashed to the curb, in his rented German car, with loud horn, so the Poles would make way for him. We hopped in and he screeched off to our hotel, laughing since.

"When you ask the Europeans for PORcelain, what you get is the Chinese Embassy, not porceLAa china. So, we saw a lot more of Warsaw (Vashava) and that night hunted down the tiny packed, long-benched Fifty Seven-cap. recital hall and heard a world renowned pianist Bonnie had heard of play the most powerful, beautiful Chopin I would never expect to hear in a lifetime. Whenever his world tours allow, the young virtuoso would secret back home to his and Chopin's Poland to play beneath the recent Russian emperors cobblestones where few people dared to listen to, let alone perform. We could not speak the language, but who needed to speak?

"This kind of experience made me realize that even after forty years under the Russians, being raped of the technology and insulted and oppressed by occupation, those people, like Dr. Kominski in Torun, sustained their human dignity and scientific integrity on such a high plain that it was worth crying over. When we visited their library, the home room of Copernicus, Bonnie politely asked something in her errant Polish of the Stalinistic matron/director about its books and records. Instantly, the dear woman leaped to attention. Our backward, American emphasis came out as a direct order from the Kremlin that she show us everything, now! We were marched to the triple iron-barred catacombs of the sub-basement where the entire history of the world it seemed had been edited and republished for the Russian-Soviet Poles for the last four decades.

"Returning to Omaha I found [then Omaha Mayor] Hal Daub raping the Omaha libraries of money for his pet projects and cutting the libraries down to a propaganda machine for the God-fearing Christian-Right-Moral Majority, so our children would never again be subjected to J.D. Salinger, Moliere, and devils such as these. Libraries were to be replaced by private bookstores and computers to save the world from the Axis of Internet.

Director of the Torun Library and our host demonstrated
the restoration of the library system as it should be.

"Back in Torun, we were gleefully secreted to environmentally controlled rooms and shown the ancient writings of the Artisians back to the 800s A.D. We could hardly dare breathe, and then, ushered down, out, and across the plaza to one of their local community THEATRES of magnificent proportions, in the class of Omaha's

Orpheum, only a little smaller and more elegant, and then, guided through the bustling streets with stoplights that BEEPED to direct the blind patrons of the city safely through dense traffic. While we Americans were spreading insecure locker room jokes about the Poles, they could not do enough for us, a couple silly Americans who still have no second language. They would gather around our cafe table or street corner to chat and offer help, in four languages no less.

"I still love Polish. It has so much French in it, since many French royalty were asked in to run the country. Polite laughter was the Poles' response to Papa Bush's Oil Crisis war. Now that was a real joke to them. And yet, the Poles still love Americans. Well, maybe it is just that my father's family comes from Alsace Lorraine, which has been German, French, German, French, German, forever. It is Poland, the breadbasket and industrial revolution of Europe. It was just parceled off by its neighbors. No USA president melted the Cold War. It was the Poles, stupid. Ask anyone with brains, especially in Europe and USSR. That is how dental history/ research has been thwarted to fit the American Dental Association's agenda, to protect the dentist from the public. It is a calm, conscious decision that works while the State protects patients from us dentists."

Manhart's '90s junket to India was another milestone experience that he again committed to words:

"Only a week in India was hardly enough, but more profound. Bombay [Mumbai] the mass of humanity that with China may soon be our leaders, already in dentistry, and according to the *New York Times,* in medicine too. In the Pune and Loni dental schools, even nearly ten years ago and never in the USA, nor now, 50 percent of India's dentists are women. On the globe over 70 percent are. The president of the university introduced me as a dentist from Omaha, Nebraska, and insisted the audience must listen and learn, while his wife, a physical therapist, sat in the front row all day. The eminent periodontists of central India challenged my concepts with utmost courtesy and professionalism, insisting on answers, and then described their own surgery as 'bull shit! I will be telling you, periodontal surgery, it bull shit.'

"Only in India: a formal ceremony with flowers to begin the scientific presentation. Never in the USA. A periodontist who shared his lab research that dove-tailed perfectly into our blood serum studies of the '80s, rendered the calcium therapies the most advanced and efficacious in the world. Never again have I questioned this: Dr. Steg and I are working with world-class dentists in Drs. Chunawala and Kamat of India, Dr. Holland et al., in Brazil, and the team in Turkey. The *New York Times* could mention that no significant breakthrough in dental science has come from the USA, save the calcium therapies, and now, it is headed abroad, without the National Institutes of Health, Omaha, the University of Nebraska or the ADA. Well, why not? Vaccine is from India, the entire concept and practice, hundreds of years ago."

THE CYST AND SPAIN

Manhart presented some of his therapies abroad at Conseuro 2009, a juried international dental congress (convention) held in Spain by the European Federation of Conservative Dentistry. For this convention he introduced what he believes to be his greatest advance yet: the discovery and treatment of a nasal palatine cyst whose infectious drainage causes various problems in the mouth, including excess plaque buildup, bleeding, tenderness, and ultimately tooth decay and dead teeth. He has devised simple calcium treatments that can stem and reverse damage, saving teeth and improving overall oral health in the process.

"We have identified three other big causes of breakdown of teeth, loss of bone, gum infection, and the one we just designed: a methodology for the cyst problem. It may be the only true bacterial cause. In other words, debris in the mouth, plus acid and bacteria. I can no longer look at that as a major cause of decay and the breakdown of the teeth. Why? Because the source of the bacteria and the toxins is the cyst. The fact that the bacteria are in the mouth at a way too high rate is the result, not the cause. The real cause is where in the hell is that cyst coming from?" Manhart said.

Manhart asserts the cause is the cyst, which he said presents in a tell-tale way. "There's a space between the upper front teeth that is characteristic. The chances of someone having a cyst are about 95 percent if they have the space. Now that spacing has been considered innocent, no problem, it does not need treating."

Besides the spacing, other symptoms can include the affected tooth having moved and being discolored. He said the cyst can be detected via X-rays if the person examining the X-ray knows what to look for and knows how to interpret it correctly. The cyst appears as a dark mass. To the vast majority of dentists, he said, the mass is either ignored or missed or explained away as normal. But to Manhart the mass is an otherwise inexplicable presence that must be accounted for rather than taken for granted as it is now.

To those who doubt or question that the mass marks a cyst, Manhart asks, "What accounts for that thing right in the middle between the roots of those teeth? You would have to have either a hole in your lip or a hole in your bone to give us that view of a darkness there." He said the reason why the cyst is not detected or why the dark mass it appears as is attributed to some benign hereditary feature is explained by dental training that turns a blind eye to the feature. From his perspective, "Nobody has given an appropriate answer to the question, *Why is that dark area there?*"

The implications of a cyst there are manifold. "Take a cyst that is a centimeter round in the front of your mouth, up under your lip, and it is draining into your mouth, not a little bit, but constantly," he said. "It is a constant drainage, and you see the after-effect twenty years later. Well, if the cyst is there and it stays there long enough, usually it might take ten or twenty years, it kills one of the teeth and so the tooth dies and becomes a source of infection in itself. And the cyst is a source of infection also, and those two things drain in the mouth.

"A comparative would be if you have a cyst draining in your arm of about the size of an almond. If that cyst were in your arm draining for ten years, you would have been going absolutely insane trying to figure out what is going on with it, and you certainly would have it fixed. You would not leave it set."

For Manhart, the cyst and the dead tooth are both an indicator and cause of persistent or recurring dental problems that many patients present. "It is as if you have the deviation or the space, there is a very high chance of having a cyst. With a cyst and a dead tooth there is about a 90 percent chance they are going to spend the rest of their life in a dental chair for all kinds of decay, all kinds of problems."

For dentists not treating the cyst, he said, "It is so frustrating to do all of this dental work and fail because everything keeps failing and you keep seeing recurring decay. That is because the cause is still there." He said the questions more dentists need to ask themselves are these: *Why does this patient always need dental care? Why is this patient's decay rate so high?*

The old standby rationales used to account for these problems no longer satisfy Manhart.

"A lot of that does not make sense anymore to me because these are adult patients; they are eating good, clean food; they are taking good care of their teeth; they are going to the dentist every four months or every six months. Yet I see a group of eight or nine patients, like I did once in California for a clinic, with a history of extensive dental care, with crowns and fillings all over their mouth, and yet they had just wild gum infection. How can that be? What is behind this? This just should not be happening," he said.

"We are finding out what is behind that, and it is the most logical answer I have ever come up with. Because when you say, 'Oh, it's hereditary, it runs in the family,' that is no good answer anymore, that is not enough anymore. 'You do not get your teeth cleaned often enough' is another reason given. No, that is not an acceptable answer. Or 'You do not know how to brush your teeth or you are eating something that is ruining your teeth.' That is not an acceptable answer anymore," he said.

"When you look at the answers we have been kind of indoctrinated with, they just do not add up. To have that big a problem in your mouth just cannot be caused by drinking a few pops a day, and I have to say that is even true of teenagers who drink too much pop, because the saliva in your mouth is so efficient, it can neutralize the mouth in just minutes. There has to be something deeper, and I have never come up with any idea that answers this as well as the cyst theory," he postulated.

He said the cyst problem is one that goes undetected by almost all dentists and physicians. "The cysts are out there and they are seen every day by every dentist. See the space between there?" he said, pointing to an X-ray of front teeth with a subtle space between them. "That is a problem with the cyst and that is the most obvious sign of that problem." He then held up an after picture of the same teeth with the space closed by crowns or braces, saying, "This is the repair, but nothing whatsoever was done about that cyst, and that cyst will drain into the mouth for the next forty years on that patient and dentists treating the person will wonder why that patient still has constant dental work to be done.

"One of the ways we miss treating this cyst problem is we straighten the teeth and so we hide it. We think there is nothing there but there is, there is a dead tooth and a cyst. I have started collecting these," he said, clutching articles clipped from dental journals, "as illustrations of dentists totally missing the point, totally missing the fact that that space up there is not a genetic thing that just occurs because your grandmother had it, and it does not occur just because you are human, and it is innocent and there is no treatment for it. This unilateral diversion here is caused by something or there has to be a reason for that to have moved in that way."

Other than his deductions, what definitive proof can Manhart offer that the nasal palatine cyst or incisal cyst exists? Only hundreds of cases and the results he has achieved. That means he is pretty much alone out there on this one.

"That is exactly right," he confirmed. How might he prove it? "Well, the most invasive way and probably the dumbest way would be to go in and cut through there and take a sample of that tissue," he said. "A more intelligent way would be to treat it and see what happens. A way that every dentist could treat it and figure it out, and it is the most accurate way, is to take and test those two teeth for vitality, by putting cold on them. That is the most accurate and the easiest way to do that. If there is a dead tooth there, you have to give me an answer why that tooth died for no apparent reason. Then what you might do is do the root canal on that tooth and see if it heals. Guess what, it does not heal. In fact, we have figured out that if you take the tooth out it does not heal, and by that I mean if it heals then that dark area should get light like regular bone. Give it six months to a year, it does not. If you leave it, it does not.

"Another very accurate way, if you have tartar right here on the lower front teeth, why does that tartar collect there? There has to be a logical reason for it collecting here as opposed to everywhere else in the mouth at the same rate. There is not a logical answer to that. The answer we have been told is not logical. We have been told there is a gland here behind the chin that dumps right in the back of those teeth, and it gives off a lot of saliva every time you eat and therefore that causes the tartar to collect. That does not make sense because the more saliva you have in your mouth, the better the buffer is to tartar collection and decay and everything. It is the great buffer of the mouth. Excessive saliva should mean less tartar, and that you do not have to prove. If you do not understand that, you don't understand biology. There are too many scientific studies that show this and that show that with the lack of saliva you have all kinds of trouble," he said.

He feels his theory explains the dead tooth syndrome and the excess tartar buildup. "The likelihood of a cyst draining right into that area makes a helluva lot more sense than the other reason because if you treat this like we treat it and get the results we get, which is to do the root canal, treat the cyst, and then find that after collecting tartar here for twenty years the tartar does not collect. Now that is very scientific research and it is long-term research."

What would a medical doctor think of his assertion about the cyst's presence and its supposed effects? Would a physician identify a cyst the way he has? "They probably would see the same dark area and interpret it the same way," he said, adding though that instead of saying it indicates a need for treatment, they would conclude the cyst does not since dentists find that that dark mass is always there. "And I am sure that dentists and physicians find it is there so often and rarely does a patient complain about any pain. Nobody goes through a lot of pain, and so therefore they deduce it must be harmless."

Manhart said the fact that the cyst is so common and that it is seemingly such a benign condition makes it hard to detect and masks its long-term and widespread damaging effects. "No one goes through a lot of pain because it is so gradual as it is draining and their tolerance level goes up so high that it does not hurt them unless something were to stop the drainage and then it flares up and becomes a huge problem. The tooth might then be taken out and surgery done, but that is like thirty years too late. And so physicians and dentists would say unless there is a lot more there, it is not a problem. Like we saw a lady one day and her tooth was out here," he indicated jutting from her mouth, "and they were talking about taking out all those teeth, but they did not mention the fact there was a cause—a cyst.

"The discoveries we have made about the cyst up here in the anterior are striking when you really look at it from a rational, common-sense way. When we get through treating somebody for the cyst—it might take six months or a year—after that they come back every six months just like you were going to any dentist and there is nothing there to do hardly at all. There is no tartar, there is no stain, they are in such great health that it takes us on the average six to seven minutes to examine and clean their teeth. If you go to a hygienist anywhere in this world to clean your teeth, it takes thirty to forty minutes. It does not make any sense at all, and to say what we are doing is silly or is just somebody's opinion is really ridiculous because this is not like every tenth case," he said. "This is like every nine and a half cases out of ten that we get these results."

His treatment for the cyst is as quick and easy and pain-free as his other treatments.

"It takes about three minutes, even without Novocain, and we do that once a month for about eight to ten months, and we will heal the cyst and the cyst will no longer be draining and your whole mouth will stay better. If two years from now we had to treat it again a little, we could, but the important thing is everything gets better for a *long* time. And when we treat people, whether we do it for the cyst or the whole mouth, and do that a couple times, the first thing they say is, 'My gums don't hurt.' Then they say things like, 'My teeth are not sensitive,'" as he described their reactions.

"Another thing we would do is check the bite to make sure that the dental work that the person has functions properly, and if it does not, you can adjust it very easily. No Novocain or anything, you do not ruin anything, you do not change anything, except how the teeth bite. Once we have got the bite right, we have got the cyst under control, the root canal done, the chances of you going for five years, ten years without any dental infection is superb. It is amazing how long this works."

Manhart is aware that he can sound a bit like a too-good-to-be-true, snake oil salesman at times. That is unavoidable given the outsider position he has been cast in. His is the lone voice raised to a loud pitch to try and be heard over the din of the dental establishment's group-speak. Occasionally, he still finds an open forum outside his office and the virtual world of cyber space when he can freely express his ideas without fear of being shouted down. One such forum was the dental congress in Spain. His presentation there about the cyst problem was entitled the Calcium Method of Osseo-Endo-Cystic Therapy. *Osseo Hundreds of dentists all over Europe now have access to this therapeutic treatment because of his appearance at the conference.

"It was held in the best hotel of Seville. It is every two years. It is for the whole continent of Europe and the Middle East. Two years ago it was in Athens, Greece. In 2011 it will be in Istanbul, Turkey. I hope to be there. Just to present something, you express interest, they send you an application, you have to write about a three-hundred-word abstract with references of what you are going to present. Then that has to go through their scientific committee for approval, which is a much more rigorous process than applying to present in the United States." He said in the U.S. all the conference organizers need to know is your credentials and the title of your proposed presentation.

At the Conseuro Congress, he said, "The whole emphasis is on conservative dentistry, preventive dentistry, periodontal, endodontics, operative materials. In other words, it is really about the parts of dentistry the general dentist has to know and has to focus on. It is not about orthodontics, it is not about oral surgery, that kind of thing. It is kind of about the nuts and bolts of general dentistry," which he said accounts for the vast majority of dentistry anywhere in the world. He said whereas in the U.S. "about 60 percent of conventions focus on the selling of dentistry, over there it is just the opposite. Clinicians present what we call clinics and what they call posters."

He said, "You really could see where European and Middle Eastern dental science comes from. It comes from the ground up because in those presentations I gave, for example, you had young dentists, old dentists, dentists doing work with dental companies, dentists in schools, students in school. It is like a groundswell. And I have never had that impression out of dentistry in this country. In fact, when I started in the '70s giving my small presentations, people would ask, 'What the hell are you going to the convention wasting your time with that?' It is kind of like we start from the top down and in Europe they start from the bottom up."

Manhart has seen enough of dentistry around the globe that he knows another thing skewed about the way the profession operates in America: its dominance by men here, although females now compose 50 percent or better of entering dental students. Women in American dental association leadership positions is another thing. His point is that the feminization of American dentistry has lagged far behind that of other developed nations, where women have long made up the majority of dentists.

"A striking thing about going to the European convention is that there are so many women dentists, because 70 percent of the dentists in Europe are women. Despite the great liberalization of American dental associations, they are still dominated severely by men," he said, which he interprets as just another manifestation of the old boys' network at work here.

Getting accepted to present at the dental congress in Spain was just one part of the juried format. After being approved he then found himself flung in a competition at the actual event. "You present for about two and a half hours. If you are interesting enough, you are presenting to about fifteen to twenty dentists at a time, maybe more," he said. The actual presentation is maybe ten to fifteen minutes, but presenters repeat it several times to dentists filtering through the convention space. "For the competition you are judged on your content, your presentation. In Chicago that is how I became a dentist who was asked back."

The competition in Spain was for a cash prize of euros. The winning presentations were made to the general assembly. Manhart's presentation was not awarded a prize but he received positive feedback. "I was told by three officials afterwards who were helping run the place that people really liked what I presented." After making his presentation a dozen times, he said he was spent. "I went back to the hotel and just collapsed."

He was impressed by the audience his nasal palatine cyst presentation drew. "They asked very, very intelligent questions. They were very drawn to it because they had never heard of this kind of thing and they wanted to know more." Even specialists. Instead of rejecting it outright, as specialists in the U.S. do, he said the international specialists "were open-minded to it." He said several specialists pulled him aside when he was done to ask him some probing questions. "They wanted me to explain things more in-depth."

"I said in my presentation, 'If you are an orthodontist, probably 60 percent of your patients have this cyst problem and you do not even see it.'" To illustrate this he mounted a display poster with an image of an X-ray showing the cyst, which appears as a dark shadow, and asked audience members to identify it. "They could not even detect the problem displayed there. They just stared at it," he said. It is a demonstration he has used with dentists in the U.S. as well, most notably with a group of dentists in New York a few years ago, and he invariably gets the same lack of recognition even though the cyst appears right before their very eyes. He said dentists and physicians cannot see it because they are not trained to see it.

The poster with the X-ray of the cyst on it was the only visual aid Manhart employed in Spain because, he said, the convention bans clever media. "They are interested in the science; they are not interested in the whistles and bells and baubles that attract people."

In addition to its serious tone, he said the convention welcomed him in an unconditional manner, unlike at American conventions where he and his ideas are often marginalized. "I was treated very, very professionally, also courteously. We were all equals there. I had an orthodontist talking to me as a general practitioner wanting to know what we can learn from each other as opposed to periodontists in America who know everything and cop the attitude, *Who the hell do you think you are telling me something I don't know in my field?* I got so tired of that paternalistic, arrogant attitude going around this country that that is one of the principal reasons I quit going [to American dental confabs]. When you go to Europe or Asia and you are treated as an equal, it is terrific."

Instead of the defensiveness and outright hostility he gets here from specialists, European specialists have time and time again accorded him his say—in Poland, in India, and most recently in Spain and France.

In the fall of 2009 he and his better half traveled to the south of France at the invitation of a leading proponent of alternative medicine on the French Riviera. Mark and Bonnie presented the cyst and skin lotion findings to a receptive group of alternative medicine practitioners. He said alternative medicine adherents at home and abroad are showing increasing interest in his calcium therapies. Despite the fact he and Bonnie practically spoke no French and their captive audience spoke broken English at best, a common language of holistic healing bridged the language gap. To Manhart's delight if not surprise, the audience unconditionally embraced what he and Bonnie had to say.

"They really got it. They were really impressed with everything," said Manhart. "We had planned to speak about two hours, and four and a half hours later we finally finished. Some of those folks we presented to are now ordering materials. I have encouraged them to take it and sell it to their own clients or their own patients if it applies to their practice, and some of it does."

As he did in Spain, he enjoyed the high level of discourse about his work that ensued in France. "Some of the questions they asked us in France were very direct. They knew what they were talking about and what we were talking about, so it was an intelligent conversation," he said. "These people are not blinded by dentists who tell us things are this and that. Just like in Spain, it was profound again how these people are so far down the road from the United States. The dentistry and medicine in Europe is so far ahead of ours."

All of which has encouraged Manhart enough that he is looking forward to future trips abroad. He described the whole experience as a breath of fresh air. "Oh God, I came home thinking I have got to go back. That exhilaration of dealing with people who are really professional and really interested in the science of what is going on as opposed to how can I make more money and sell more dentistry was refreshing. The whole thing about going to other countries is that it is such a great way to get back into organized dentistry, kind of by the side door."

He and Bonnie may be going to India again as a follow-up to the trip they made there in the 1990s. Manhart is excited by the prospect of introducing a new generation of dentists to his methodologies.

He is equally excited by the prospect of his calcium products being distributed and sold around the world. He is in preliminary negotiations with someone in France to do just that. "That is another side door," said Manhart. "I just love the idea of being able to go to someplace like that and spend the money and the time and know it is really going to be valuable." He is also training some dentists in England via the Internet. All these contacts in Europe, he said, grew out of the conference in Spain.

He is writing a full scientific paper based on the last thirty years of his work for submission to a European journal. The paper will lay out the methodology of his Calcium Method of Osseo-Endo-Cystic Therapy. "They may be open to it because they were very open to a smaller paper of mine they published before," he said.

The more doors Manhart opens, the more opportunities there are.

He describes Osseo-Endo-Cystic Therapy as "our latest breakthrough. Spain was the icing on the cake. But that whole thing is just exploding. We are finding the need for it in so many people. We now see over fifty cases a month and that is a conservative estimate."

He said the more he and his partner Dr. Steg have looked into the cyst question, the more they have come to know that "the cells are there in utero." In other words, people are born with the biological or cellular substrate of the cyst. "And something happens that initiates those cells to start giving off toxins and growing and forming a duct to dump the toxins right into the mouth."

He believes excessive dental work is one culprit that initiates the sequence. "It could be orthodontics, it could be cleaning the teeth or crowning the teeth in that area," he said. "We figure the cyst develops in over 50 percent of the dental population. It is a heckuva problem." He further believes that most failed orthodontic work could be explained by the cyst factor. His therapeutic approach to treating the problem is one he would like to see more dentists adopt.

MANHART AND THE ESTABLISHMENT

He has made what he considers a series of significant discoveries, but the more he has tried advancing his ideas within the American dental community, the more roadblocks he has had put in his way. Manhart being Manhart, however, he is not about to let anyone or anything stop him from pushing forward.

Being a scientific explorer, which is how he thinks of himself to a large degree, means postulating, hypothesizing, investigating, experimenting, studying, quantifying, and applying his methodologies and eating the cost. That is just his makeup. Thus, much of his work in calcium he has funded himself, out of his own pocket. Not for lack of trying to secure research backing. But being a maverick general practitioner, rather than a specialist or a trained laboratory technician, has meant he has had to do his investigatory work on his own or under the radar, sometimes circumventing normal channels. Even those times he has tried playing the game by all the rules he feels he has been sabotaged, his work thwarted, stalled, dismissed, rejected.

"One of the big disadvantages of organized dentistry is that it is so organized and so

insulated from people who do not belong to the club that what we have done is walled ourselves off from a whole segment that is just as valuable if not more valuable," he said. "In other words if you are under the umbrella, you may not get rained on, but you may not get water you need to grow, and that is kind of an analogy I think of. You need the water, you need the people who can nourish you with new ideas."

"I was told this by a Creighton endodontist when I got muscled out of teaching: 'Well, Mark, now you can think on your own.' There is a lot of truth to that. The dentists even admit to this. They will not do anything new until it is safe and does not disturb the stability of income and safe means approved by enough of organized dentistry, like the schools, the associations, and the whole thing ends up a fail-safe way of protecting income," he said.

"So many dentists have responded over the years to what we are doing as if they were going to lose money doing this, and I think in a sense some will but in the long run of a normal practice it is actually a money-saver and a money-making thing that helps people, and the more you help people, the more accepted you are as a dentist."

He believes a major weakness of American dental training is how unprepared new dentists are when they enter the field fresh from the insulated academic world.

"They do not understand business because the whole cycle of becoming a dentist is that you get out of college, where you have already been really protected from life there most of the time. You have not really lived much of life, unless you are older. Then you go to professional school and you have not really lived much life there. Then you get out of it and go right into practice," he explained.

A newly practicing dentist, he said, then becomes beholden to the American Dental Association. "Organized dentistry has a stranglehold on dentists and it comes out in numbers. About 70 percent of dentists belong to the American Dental Association; whereas, only 30 percent of physicians even bother joining the American Medical Association. You can practice medicine and who cares whether you are in the AMA, you are in your own thing, you are free to do what you want, and so the AMA does not have this stranglehold on physicians," he said.

The way he sees it, the ADA stranglehold is three-tiered: at the national, state, and local levels. He said the organization is merely a professional association and has no regulatory or licensing authority.

"It is like joining a frat, that is all it is. I call it a yacht club because in dentistry it is so easy to rape the public. I mean, it is so easy, and some dentists brag about it. We are almost taught to be greedy. It is terrible. And yet the ADA actually acts like they run our profession and that is something I used to really believe in—that they should, until I realized the only reason they are in existence is to protect the dentist from the patient. Well, that is the job of government, which the government does. The state protects the patient from the dentist and that is very healthy. But the other is not healthy at all because it becomes such a closed society. It is the best union in this country," he said. Because of this tail-wagging-the-dog structure, he said, "We are probably the most unregulated profession."

He finds it distasteful and dangerous that dentists use the ADA to protect themselves from patients. His disdain for the ADA led him to cut ties with it some time ago. For a long time he was a rising star in the ADA. "I was even asked to go to training sessions to become a big wheel in the American Dental Association, and I could have if I had been a good boy."

His breaking ranks with the ADA and his public criticism of it and of his profession make him and the way he practices dentistry the antithesis of organized dentistry. "And that is why I am in the position I am in right now," he said, meaning on the outside looking in. "There may not be a lot of dentists who think real highly of me, but having been in this position of being on our own, we have learned more than we ever could have possibly have learned by following all the rules and getting in lock step with everybody else, because your creative thinking just goes ... poof! It is like it is sucked right out of you. It is not in the profession."

Whatever discouragement he has felt from his profession has not been enough to make him throw up his hands and quit, even though there have been times when he may have been tempted to. When push comes to shove, though, a Manhart does not give in. At least not this Manhart. Just as stubbornness and persistence are family traits, he believes the ingenuity and curiosity genes run "in the family."

He explained: "I remember when I was a really little kid, my brothers Paul and David, who were probably teenagers at the time, took apart my dad's Lincoln [automobile] to fix it, and they could not get it all back together. It's like they had pieces left over. My brother David, he's the fourth oldest, has always had a very creative mind and an intuition of invention, and I am sure he got it from Dad.

"It is just that so much of what he [David] would talk about could not be put into practical application. I can always remember him talking about, for example, 'these damn interstate highways they are putting in' and how 'they are going to cause so much pollution. It will cause so much smoke around cities and even along highway corridors. It will be terrible and we're going to have big problems with our air.' He did not have all the correct words, but Dave was always into that whole environmental-ecological focus. But when somebody in the '50s was saying this to you, well, a lot of people thought he was a real kook. At family functions I usually found myself sitting and talking with Dave more than anybody else," Manhart remembers. "He is old and frail now but he was so profoundly correct about what was coming, and we ridiculed him. I am glad to have listened as much as I did as a kid."

Just as Manhart ended up a chip off the old block by becoming a professional and inventor like his father, he has come to view his brothers John and David as kindred spirits. They are all thinkers, dreamers, and doers. Eccentrics in a way, too. That same iconoclastic spirit guided the brothers' father. Old man Manhart's law practice was downtown until he moved operations to the family home.

"He took a part of the house and used it as his office, and that was really rather unusual in those days," said Manhart, who is known to do some calcium applications at his home. Like it or not, we all become our parents to one degree or another, and Manhart seems to have taken after his old man in any number of ways, which is something he takes pride in because of how much he admired his father.

6

Finding a Way, Going on His Own

OMAHA

By the time Manhart's father got settled in his law practice in the Roaring Twenties, Omaha was already a bustling city of some quarter million residents with a dynamic downtown and an economy largely based on railroad, livestock, agribusiness, insurance, and manufacturing. When Mark Manhart started his dentistry practice forty years later on the twelfth floor of the Medical Arts Building at 17th and Dodge, the city's economic base was quite similar, but big changes were on the horizon. By the late '60s and early '70s the meatpacking plants that employed many thousands of workers began to close. Within two decades the once mammoth Omaha Stockyards was on its way out. Omaha transitioned into a white-collar telecommunications and data processing center.

The biggest physical change is how the city's dimensions grew. When Manhart was a boy, Omaha's city limits barely reached past 60th Street. He "went out of town" to work at a gas station at 72nd and West Dodge Road. He remembers how the Philly's gas station would shake when the semis barreled by. Even when he was first practicing, Omaha's westernmost borders extended only to 72nd Street. Beyond that were open fields and farmland. Suburban sprawl touched off a development boom in the '60s that is still under way. Omaha now stretches well past 200th Street on its western boundaries.

The opposite end of Omaha is its riverfront, which for years remained inaccessible to the public due to a heavy industrial infrastructure that contaminated the water and soil and presented an ugly footprint and first impression to folks flying over or driving through on the river side. It is only in the last decade the city has realized its long-envisioned Back to the River dream with a spate of clean-up and redevelopment that has transformed the riverfront into pleasing public spaces where people reside, work, dine, recreate, celebrate. As Omaha looked west, Manhart bucked the trend to stay downtown, practicing there for years in the Medical Arts Building and later in the nearby Old Market.

A city that has struggled to find a marketable image is finally coming out of its shell and branding itself a sophisticated urban setting. Not nearly as densely populated as other big cities, Omaha has grown by spreading out rather than filling in, although there are signs the sprawl is slowing and an inner-city revitalization is gaining momentum. The state's liberal annexation laws and the city's aggressive annexation policies have added dozens of communities and subdivisions to the Omaha tax rolls, helping Omaha grow even as many of its native sons and daughters have left. The Manharts have done their part to keep Omaha thriving by mostly staying put and thereby contributing a large extended family to the city rolls. With a population well in excess of four hundred thousand and a metro area tally of more than eight hundred fifty thousand, Omaha is a major urban player today that is headquarters to four Fortune 500 companies and home to a world-class attraction in the Henry Doorly Zoo, whose annual attendance now approaches two million.

Nebraska has a tiny populace that has experienced only a negligble net gain in recent years as many small towns have withered and died and others are struggling to stay alive. The state's economy was once built on family farms and factories, but those kinds of jobs are becoming scarce in the new service industry economy. Nebraska suffers from the so-called brain drain effect that sees many residents leave, taking their time, talent, and treasure with them, for seemingly better educational, employment, and quality of life opportunities or amenities elsewhere. A state with a small labor force and tax base to draw on can hardly afford to lose its best and brightest. Whether or not Nebraska can stem the tide of expatriates remains to be seen.

THE AIR FORCE AND ALASKA

Manhart could have joined the exodus of those who left. Well, he did for a time, when he joined the Air Force after taking his dental degree in 1962 and wound up stationed in Anchorage, Alaska. He considers his time in uniform a baptism by fire that not only accelerated his progress as a dentist but his development as a human being.

He said, "I learned so much dentistry so damn fast in the Air Force. It was like dental school in six months because of what you learned from those dentists who were from other parts of the country and especially the ones who were dentists in the Air Force as a career. It was like, 'Hey, let's start over here and learn real dentistry.'"

The Air Force appealed to his sense of wanderlust. He was a young man on the move who went right from getting his prerequisite studies in three years of college to earning his dental license to entering the military. Before he knew it, he was an officer (captain) honing his craft, seeing the world, and making a decent pay grade. Good thing, too, because he had serious responsibilities to take care of, as in a family, at an age when many new college grads and young officers are still in party mode. He and his first wife, Mary, got married while he was still in school.

Note: He returned to college part-time in the 1970s and finally finished his bachelor of science degree at age fifty-one in 1988.

"We had one kid and one on the way by the time I left Creighton for the Air Force," he said. He was already heavily in debt, too. He had taken a loan out and the couple had help from their folks. "Mary's folks helped us get a little house to live in at 36th and California." To help make ends meet, he had worked summers and earlier times at a North Omaha tool and die factory making hydraulic motors. Once accepted to dental school he quit working the manufacturing job because he saw one too many people injure their hands, which were going to be his livelihood, after all. "I had to tell Dad, 'That's it, I'm not going to work in the factory anymore,'" he said.

"Later, it was a real compliment to get into the Air Force because you just don't walk into it. You can't just say, I want to be in the Air Force. You didn't then and you don't now. You have to pass intellectually and physically. I didn't think I had any problem getting in. I mean, I had the education and I had the background. I was not a real brilliant guy by any means, but I guess they figured if you can get through dental school, you can get into the Air Force, and not only get out, but honorably," according to Manhart.

His wife was initially taken aback when he opted for the service but soon saw it as he did as a gateway to travel and adventure. "I think she was kind of struck by it at first, but we had talked a lot about what we wanted, and we decided an assignment overseas would be a great way to see the world, so I volunteered overseas," he said. "We figured that would be good. We were hoping to go to Europe. But, you know, you do not get to do what you want to do in the service, you do what you are told or you get your butt kicked."

His in-laws were slower to come around. "I know Mary's folks were really not in favor because she was leaving. She was one of three kids, but they accepted it."

For Manhart the service offered a sweet deal. Most importantly, it offered a stable income to support his young family. Had he been in civilian practice there was no guarantee he could match the service pay just starting out on his own. "You go into the Air Force and you get paid every month. It is very good pay, it's a very good rank, you are a captain, you are an officer, so you are a select group right there. Plus, I got extra pay for the overseas duty, " he said.

Then there was the fact it offered him the advantage of furthering his dental skills by working alongside veteran dentists with years of experience and refined techniques and all without the pressure of having to bring in business by cultivating and retaining patients. "Another reason is you get to practice and you do not have to build a practice. I mean, in a sense you do not have to have responsibility for people like you do in your own practice. That cuts two ways. You do not have to have responsibility toward the patient because they might leave you, but when you are in the service and you do not do a halfway decent job and the CO finds out about it, you can get your butt kicked again. There are consequences to that," he said.

He acknowledges that the promise of a sure thing inside the Air Force versus the risk of setting up his own practice on the outside made the military an attractive option. But it is not like he did not have a ready-made patient roll waiting for him back home. No, the military was as much about a chance for a fresh start, a new horizon as it was anything else.

"Maybe it was insecurity in a sense," he wondered. "Then again, I knew I could be successful because I had such a big family. If I just worked on my family and friends alone, I would make enough. It would not be any problem. All you have to do is be a good boy, be in the right church, and, you know, hang around with your family and friends all the time. Well, I did not get a big kick out of that idea. I was not sure I wanted to really stay in Omaha. Besides, my wife and I wanted to try something really different."

Alaska was not exactly what they had in mind. Technically, it is not overseas. But it certainly qualified as a change of scenery that was really different. The extreme cold necessitates doing all sorts of things differently than the way you are used to.

"Most of the year there to wash your car you set it in the rare sun, washed one side with warm water, then turned it around with the other side to the sun and washed it," he said. "Plugging in the car's block heater was routine, even during the day. Wet skin on metal was a 'No, no, let go.'"

Walking even a short distance in a winter storm in Alaska is inadvisable unless you are tethered. The white-out conditions and dangerous cold and wind are nothing to fool with.

Of course, the weather in Alaska is not always so treacherous. There are moderate, temperate stretches. The couple spent three years there, and it proved to be some of the happiest years of their married life. They made the most of getting out and enjoying the natural wilderness and scenic beauty surrounding them.

His one and only hunting excursion in Alaska and the story of what happened to a pair of colleagues during their own hunting trip on the frozen tundra dampened his enthusiasm for the sport. He wrote down his recollection of those events:

"Two things while in Alaska pushed me away from the adventuresome. At a remote site I went hunting bear with an armed sportsman on one side of a valley wilderness. Shots rang out and whistled by us. Before we could take cover more shots came too close, so our guide fired back and took a look in his glasses. Across the valley were other armed hunters of bear who must have realized bears do not carry firearms, nor do they shoot back. That was it for me, especially when we had returned to the base and I asked 'What is a 'sound shot?'"

The reply was simple and insane, 'Oh, that's when you hear a noise, you shoot.' Like our dear former vice president [Dick] Cheney, right?

"The second was the tale of two California classmate dentists and the Big Horn Rack. The two were guided up the Alaskan range to bring down a big-horned Siberian sheep for each of their future dental offices. After a day's climb the safari was already a big bang success as they spied the sheep out in the open. The guide whispered that they would get only one shot, so take aim, and on the count of three, fire. They did, BANG! One sheep dropped as the rest vanished forever. I have no idea who got the gigantic rack, maybe one horn each, but never again would the two dentists speak, maybe not even yet."

Deciding that his own close call and the potential for a feud were too heavy a price to pay for enjoying the great outdoors, Manhart settled on fishing as his communion with nature. Even that sport poses its own hazards in those unforgiving environs. Out on the water in an open boat always presents the risk of capsizing or falling overboard and even a couple minutes exposure in those frigid waters can be fatal.

Meanwhile, Manhart found himself steeped in the latest dental methods and practices while assigned to Elmendorf Air Force Base in Anchorage. He was continually learning new things. "It was a big clinic with about thirty dentists. You cannot help but learn from thirty dentists from all over the country. Professionally, being on Elmendorf Air Force

Base was perfect: a large dental clinic, a hospital clinic, the remote clinics on the Air Force sites all over the state, and the responsibility to work under a schedule where you had to plan your time and procedures to keep up or get moved to a nothing position."

Dental corpsmen in Alaska practiced an extreme form of dentistry befitting the locale's rugged, wild-and-woolly conditions. "This was my first and last chance to do dentistry out of a portable high-speed briefcase while in mukluks and a hooded parka," he said. "If you kept your hands in the patient's mouth and worked damned fast, it was easy. It was a great situation to learn real dentistry under the pressure of time and quality. It seems I learned more dentistry in that first year in the United States Air Force Dental Corps than in the four years in school.

"My first day there started in the CO's office where he made it clear I was replacing Dr. Carl Ritola from Wyoming, who wore Big Shoes. My favorite dentist was a Mormon fellow, Dr. Wilber Rowner, who was kind of a rebel." The more-experienced Rowner routinely "was getting his work done in a third or a half the time, all the time," compared to everyone else. "It took us almost an hour to get a tooth filled and he was done and out of that office in twenty minutes." Manhart being a green-from-college inductee could only look on in awe. For that matter, his fellow rookie dentists were amazed by the speed and efficiency that "Dr. Wilber," as his patients called him, displayed.

Then, Manhart suddenly found himself on the spot when the Commanding Officer ordered him "to check" Rowner's work while the dentist was on temporary leave. The CO suspected Dr. Wilber was shirking his duty because he was getting his work done so fast and had so much time to relax between patients. "Something's going on here and we have got to find out what it is," Manhart was told.

"So, Wilber goes on vacation and I go into his office and take his patients and all the patients say, 'Where's Dr. Wilber? We want to see Dr. Wilber.' After a couple days I had to report to the commander that he had better lay off Wilber because his patients loved him and his dental work was so good I could not touch its quality. It was like dentistry that took us ten years to learn," Manhart said.

Being privy to that advanced, master-level work in such an intense, concentrated way gave Manhart the kind of accelerated training, he said, "I never would have received in Omaha. Where we were taught in dental school to do a denture in sixteen steps, these guys could do it in three, and they would make a better denture because most of what they were doing was in their head [ingrained to the point that it was muscle memory]. And so I learned how to make a denture in three or four steps."

Manhart and Mary became friends with Wilber and his wife, Zoe, and their seven girls. The two men would trade good-natured jibes about their respective religious faiths. To Manhart the Mormon religion "seemed like a fairy-tale for children," and Wilber told Manhart he felt the same way about Catholicism. Not more than a decade later Manhart would, as he terms it, "put away the things of a child" and distance himself from Catholicism or any organized religion.

In military as in civilian life not all patients have the same rank or status. It should not make a difference in the quality of care patients receive or in how they are treated, but try telling that to an officer. Manhart got his first taste of what it is like to deal with a demanding patient who is used to calling the shots when a general sat in his chair.

"You know when the general comes in, everything goes right. I just got picked to work on him, and as I turned around with the needle in hand to give him an injection," he said, 'What the hell are you doing? I am allergic to that.' It was kind of embarrassing, so I turned around and looked at his chart and there was no record about being allergic to anesthesia. I said, 'General, I am sorry but there is nothing here that says you are allergic to this.' The general barked, 'Goddamn, what are you talking about?' He was really pissed.

"Boy, I know that somebody lost something [as in a rank or promotion] over that. He grabbed the chart and he could not find any record of it either. I said, 'It's important that we mark this down' and he said, 'Well, I am a general, I do not need to have this written down. Everybody knows that.' I said, 'Well, you might be in combat and somebody doesn't know you are allergic to it and uses it on you.' Oh, he got pissed again."

Manhart's insistence must have made an impression though because, he said, "that led to the general's wife coming in and my working on her. She sent me a very nice thank you note, which I still have."

During Manhart's time in the service (1963 to 1965) America was embroiled in the Cold War on many fronts. American troops were perpetually in force and on alert in Germany, Korea, Japan, and Guantanamo Bay. The nation's strategic defense was largely based just outside Omaha, at Offutt Air Force Base, the home for the then–Strategic Air Command, in Bellevue, Nebraska. A year before he entered the service, the Cuban missile crisis brought the U.S. and Soviet Union to the brink of World War III.

A year later President John F. Kennedy was assassinated, sparking new doubts and anxieties about the nation's future. By the time Manhart left the Air Force a long-simmering conflict in Southeast Asia had become a full-blown war. America was sending an ever-increasing number of military personnel to Vietnam, whose name few Americans had ever heard of and whose location even fewer could identify on a globe. Though the jungle and rice paddy warfare of Vietnam was a remote world away from the cold wilderness of Alaska, Manhart observed America's military escalation in a most intimate way by working on young men en route to missions in "the shit" or coming back from in-country tours of duty.

Manhart said the Elmendorf base's extreme seclusion made it an ideal jumping-off point for airmen to be funneled from the States to Vietnam and back again with hardly anybody knowing about it. Ideal in terms of U.S. government leaders and policy makers who were concealing the true extent of this nation's involvement in the war. The buildup of forces continued almost unabated through 1968.

"These airmen were rushed through the dental clinic a few hundred at a time to get anything done that would be a distraction, and to record their existing conditions," he said.

A grim reminder for Manhart of the life-and-death stakes involved was the critical part that dental work and dental records play in identifying G.I.s in the event they are killed in action. Everything has to be done quickly and done right.

"You get his X-rays in two minutes and you better not make a mistake," he said. "It did not take you long to figure out that the reason you never should make a mistake is that that guy may come back in a black body bag and then he cannot be identified. Yeah, I mean, that is how real it got. That reality hit you just so hard."

The weight of that responsibility was too much for some of Manhart's colleagues. They just could not cut the pressure. "Some guys were pulled out of that who could not do that. They got out to go do something else, because they could not live with the idea of making a mistake that prevented positive identification."

BACK HOME, STARTING PRACTICE

Despite the pressures, the military agreed with Manhart and he seriously contemplated making it a career. "We were going to stay in the Air Force. I figured if I stayed in just long enough, I could be a bird colonel and then retire and go into practice and teach. That would have been a nice thing to do. You could travel all over the world, too. But you really could not get any roots set. That was not appealing to me, and Mary did not care for that either," he said.

That is when he set his sights back on home. It is ironic that the very things that motivate people to leave a place like Omaha—namely its homey, small town, conservative, family-friendly quality—are often the very things that lure some of those same people back. Combined with its strong work ethic, low crime rate, solid schools, and abundant parks, Omaha is widely viewed, and not without justification, as a good place for setting roots down and raising a family. Manhart began sending out feelers to see where he might break in to the Omaha dental scene.

"Dr. Eugene Merchant practiced in the Medical Arts Building downtown, and he had gotten a job to be the assistant dean down at the University of Nebraska Dental School, and so I wrote him and asked if I could meet him and possibly to take his practice, to buy his practice. Well, it worked out great because I came along just at the right time. He was in a hurry because the school year was going to start. I flew back here and met him and we made the deal on a handshake and I took over his practice. He was one of the most highly respected dentists in the whole state," Manhart said.

Returning to Omaha was bittersweet. Manhart came back disheartened and disillusioned by America's growing military-industrial complex. Manhart had been shaken by America and the Soviet Union going to the brink of nuclear war during the Cuban missile crisis in October of 1962. He was up north when President Kennedy was assassinated during a motorcade through Dallas, Texas, in November 1963. Like so many people of a certain age, Manhart can remember exactly where he was and precisely what he was doing when he heard the tragic news. He was in the Elmendorf clinic filling an upper left bicuspid on an airman when the first reports came out, and then he could hardly finish the procedure through all the tears.

As far back as childhood Manhart had turned a critical eye on his country. "The atom bomb on Japan was hard to stomach. I am still trying to choke it down." As an adult Manhart began to see more clearly the folly of imperialism and nationalism. Anything that smacked of jingoistic hyperbole turned him off.

"After the Cuban missile crisis and three years in the Air Force in Alaska, our return found Omaha had not changed a wink. I had. During Vietnam I had plans to move to Canada, but by Bush I's Gulf War I was too old and had to stick it out, and we ain't out yet. About 1963 I reread Gandhi more closely and found that the cowards are the ones making the world a hellish warring place for others. They cannot follow the progress of normal human life and death," he said.

He had changed in other ways, too. While ensconced in the Great North he had become more attuned to his artistic side. He said, "I took more time studying art and painting as well as the architecture of Frank Lloyd Wright."

Rather than cut and run Manhart decided to carve out a life in Omaha. The city of his birth and coming of age would be his proving ground as a man. In a sense he was following his father's path of having gone away to find himself only to return ready to face the world. Just like his father before him had begun his law practice in downtown Omaha, Manhart began his dentistry practice (1965) downtown, the commercial center of the city where the bulk of professionals once conducted business.

Soon after his Air Force discharge Manhart took over Dr. Merchant's practice at the Medical Arts Building on South 17th Street. The building was once the premier office site in Omaha where doctors delivered their healing arts. The seventeen-story Thomas Rogers Kimball–designed building with its distinctive ornamental terra cotta facade opened in 1926.

"Hell, we were in an ideal place to practice, and the camaraderie that occurred there was completely different because I think about every one of the dentists there either stopped in the office or called or we met at lunch to say, 'Hey, great having you here, let me know if you ever need a hand,' or 'I'll call you if I need a hand.' That was great." He said that collegiality began to wane and by the late '70 stopped altogether or at least became the exception rather than the rule. "It became really rather ruthless competition."

The saying goes that all good things must come to an end. Another goes, to everything there is a season. When Omaha's Great Fathers deemed that the Medical Arts Building had outlived its usefulness, it was imploded in 1999 to make room for the One First National Center, a forty-story glass and steel tower that is Omaha's new signature high rise. Progress it is called. Omaha's spotty preservationist record must count the loss of the Medical Arts Building as a major loss. After all, the One First National Center could have been built elsewhere, without having to tear down an iconic part of the Omaha skyline. A remnant of the Medical Arts Building lives on in the One First National tower's atrium lobby in the form of a salvaged section of terra cotta. The section is displayed as a slice of nostalgic history and classic aesthetic design. Manhart hated to see his old office digs go the way of rubble and dust and memory. He would much rather have seen it preserved.

"Yes, a lot of downtown people were upset when the Medical Arts Building came down. I could not watch it. We had watched the big old Post Office Building right out our office windows come down several years earlier, and that was terrible," he remembered. "Even the original First National Bank was hard to go into until I became a 'charter member' of the Press Club and had lunch there a lot. I guess I got over those things more easily because there was so much to do at home and in the office."

He wishes he and not a physician he knows had salvaged as a keepsake the building plaque with the name Medical Arts engraved on it, but if Manhart cannot have it for himself, he is glad that someone has preserved it.

The office he opened in the Old Market—site of Omaha's late nineteenth and early twentieth century warehouse district saved from the wrecking ball by forward-thinking business leaders and artists—was his way of showing solidarity with the landmark preservation movement.

Stretching a point or not, Manhart is a die-hard preservationist when it comes to saving people's teeth as well. He prides himself on only removing teeth as a last resort. His Institute has become the treatment option of choice for many patients who have been told by other dentists that they needed drastic extractions or other oral surgery. He helps many "lost causes" not only keep their teeth and avoid needless pain but save thousands of dollars in dental bills, too. It is an "old-fashioned" concept he is glad to sustain.

"The old guys taught us to 'take the teeth to the grave.' Nothing modern dentistry has developed comes anywhere near the complex genius human nature has built for dental structures. It is a concept and human condition that has allowed me to enjoy practicing all my adult life. Now that we have discovered so much more with calcium materials, I am astounded almost every day to be part of the advancement of dental care," he said.

While he had no trouble reintegrating himself into the fabric of Omaha life after his stint in the service, he felt constrained by the city's stultifying social atmosphere. Among other things, Omaha was a racially divided community whose de facto segregation permeated every layer of society during the height of the civil rights movement. The heavy, paternalistic hand of organized religion, corporate fat cats, political machines, and military brass, courtesy the SAC headquarters, made it a conservative enclave.

A leading Omaha mover-and-shaker he got to know was Milo Bail, the president of then–Omaha University. Bail was a no-nonsense sort who ran the school with military precision. Indeed, Manhart was privy to many stories Bail told about Gen. Curtis LeMay, the original commander of SAC, whom Bail befriended. Bail enlisted the general's support in establishing a large bootstrappers program at the school that for decades served many military personnel. Manhart wrote a play, *Bootstrappers Christmas,* that is a kind of homage to the program's early years in the 1950s.

The fact that Manhart found Omaha lagging behind the times upon his return from the Air Force is not to suggest the city did not have its own expressions of the freedom struggle, the peace movement, the counter-culture scene, et cetera. It did. The De Porres Club and the 4CL carried the fight for equal rights with public protests. The Black Panthers were active on the North side. Student demonstrations led to the formation of the Department of Black Studies at the University of Nebraska at Omaha. Civil disturbances erupted in response to racist events and to the war in Vietnam. A federal lawsuit filed by a group of parents resulted in a forced busing program to integrate Omaha's public schools. The Old Market evolved into the city's hippie district filled with head shops and avant-garde art happenings.

MANHART AND MONTESSORI

Clearly, the-times-they-are-a-changin' world caught up to Omaha in some respects, it is just that to Manhart's eyes the city as a whole still seemed stuck in a status-quo insularity that was in sharp contrast to the more progressive waves seen in other parts of the nation.

"We had been gone three years and nothing in the world had changed in Omaha. I hated that," he said. "That period of the '60s was to me really a time of great revolution in this country. For me it was a great era for discovery." One of his discoveries was Montessori, the early childhood education program that he and Mary were introduced to in Alaska. "I discovered Montessori education there and I started my kids in it. I got very deeply into Montessori."

"By the time we got back to Omaha in 1965, I had read and learned firsthand a lot about it. Once, when our flight was delayed in Portland, Oregon, for a trip back home, I was able to visit a great Montessori school there run by nuns. It was quite unusual because the indoctrination and religiosity had been kept out of the program. The family and the arts were always more 'natural wonders' to us," he said.

The Montessori approach is similar to the one he used with his own kids at home. "The form of education is what you might describe as benign neglect. You let a kid grow and you watch for those periods when the kid grows in a certain area and you help them with that, and then when they change and grow, you respond to that. It is basically learning self-discipline and learning things when your mind and body are ready to learn them and use them. It is very hands-on, common sense, every day education that has transformed education all over the Western world. I have been into things like that ever since. Nobody was so ahead of her time as Dr. Maria Montessori, the Italian physician who began it all," Manhart observed.

He feels that one reason he may have been so attracted to the Montessori methodology was that it represented such a departure from the rigid rearing he experienced as a young child. "I just wanted to break free of that and allow for self-development and especially self-discipline because if there is anything that has changed, if there is anything terrible about our society's education system today," he said, "it is the lack of self-discipline, and you don't have to say any more about it."

Manhart became a regular Johnny Appleseed for Montessori. "When I got back to Omaha, my brother Hugh and I started the Omaha Montessori Society. I used to go around lecturing about its educational precepts. We brought the first Montessori teachers to Omaha. There was some friction within the Omaha group that eventually was resolved. We were very highly criticized by public educators and especially by private educators. We were accused of bringing Communism to our children and ruining children. It got distasteful at times, but to me it was terribly exciting. There are people who call me The Father of Omaha Montessori, which I really take as a compliment, and once in a while I run into the remnants of that."

MANHART, RELIGION, AND DEVELOPING HIS OWN CODE

Before his falling out with organized dentistry Manhart butted heads with organized religion. Truth be told, his association with both the dental and religious communities began amicably. He was a member in good standing of the American Dental Association and an active participant and officer in its local dental society. He was the editor and business manager of the Omaha Dental Society's journal.

Similarly, he became an ardent lay leader in the Omaha Catholic Archdiocese. But just as the rigidity of the dental establishment alienated him, the rigidity of the church left him frustrated. In his view, the laity were mere window-dressing for the church and its religious leaders.

"I got very deeply into church things and religious activity, like what was called the Archdiocesan Pastoral Council, which is supposed to help the bishop run the diocese," he said. "There were a handful of people and I was one of them. I ended up secretary of the pastoral council. We officers would meet once a month with the archbishop. This was when I was a young dentist in Omaha, and even with that I realized we were just there to talk and push pencils.

"It really hit me one time when we were talking about how to get young people involved with church and how to be of service to the community, and I said something about what was it that made the Beatles such great stars in music, why that kind of music was so good for youth, and why *Jesus Christ Superstar,* the rock opera, was so great. Well, that hit like a lead rock with the administration. I guess I should have known better than to say that," Manhart said.

On some level he suspects the ritual and pageantry and theatricality of church services appealed to his sense of drama. "Church activities really are theatrical to a great extent.

When you go to a religious rite, what you are doing is going to theatre. It is theatre. That is where theatre came from. I learned a lot from the experience of working with the church. I learned about organizational skills, how to organize groups, because we used to plan weekend religious activities [retreats], and you had to plan every five minutes of the day, and so that really gave me a sense of organization, group dynamics, and human relations that are so necessary in live theatre."

The late '60s was a time of ferment, upheaval, and experimentation both within the church and within society at large, and Manhart let himself be swept up on the tide of progressive change. He said, "There were great ideas occurring in those days with the Second Vatican Council and everything that was almost ignored around here. I found changes on the West Coast and in Alaska. Few people around here had ever heard of them. But I never got into what you would call the really extreme left or the crazies on the extreme right. It just never appealed to me. I would just as soon walk away and find something else to do than go around carrying signs."

One of the ways his evolving humanistic, world-citizen sensibilities got expressed was his traveling to a Third World nation to deliver dental care—an experience that forever changed him. It was 1971 when he went to Venezuela, South America, with Father Bill Kalin, a cousin, to visit the priest's parish in Barquisimeto, west of Caracas. Manhart was familiar with junkets or missions that dentists and doctors made to such locales, and he thought that sometimes their energies were misplaced. Instead of traveling to deliver care there through some university or association or foundation, Manhart just up and left on his own. He went with his friend Father Jim Schwertley, and the pair meet Fr. Kalin in Miami for the University of Nebraska's Orange Bowl game versus Louisiana State University, which NU won 17–12 to claim the school's first national championship. Then Mark and Fr. Kalin continued on to South America with no agenda except to help people badly in need of dental care.

Manhart put down in words some of his impressions from that trip:

"U.S. dentists would go to the Dominican Republic and spend their vacation pulling the teeth of natives. It was like a game to see who could pull the most teeth. Dumber than dumb. I always thought we should be teaching these indigenous people how to get clean water and what teeth are and why we try to save them. So, Fr. Bill and I headed for Venezuela. Caracas is and was a majestic wonder, better today than then, and Barquisimeto made Omaha seem tiny.

"In every barrio we walked into, the people knew I was El Professor, the Tooth Yanker, so the dirt streets were empty as they hid out of sight. We showed that we had no instruments or cameras and asked to come into their huts. The first thing you would see many times was a fading picture of JFK, instead of the pope or their own nation's president.

"In no time I was welcomed enough to speak at their schools, where we gave out the few toothbrushes I had brought. It was a riot to teach them how to use them, on their teeth. When I compared keeping their teeth nice to keeping their hair and eyes nice so they could see and look good, it became a laughfest with each class, as we all had fun learning. Every once in a while you could see in the eyes of a certain girl or boy a brilliance that stopped you and held on. I asked about this and the teacher would say, 'Aztec.' Then you knew you were in the presence of a natural wonder. It is a look you cannot forget."

Manhart relished this immersion in another culture and the fresh perspective it gave him on institutional oppression of the poor. Here are some more scattered impressions from his South American sojourn, including some erudite, caustic observations:

"Coke cut a deal to make their pop cheaper than milk so they could sell more. The fresh bread was mana from heaven. Jesuits would flunk their final exams for advanced degrees, so they had to continue working in the barrios instead of being assigned to work with the wealthy students. Now that is revolution I can go with. Ninety-eight percent of the wealth was in the hands of 2 percent of the people blessed by the Catholic church, a perfect set-up for eternal despotism and religious fanaticism. That is why common sense Communism flourishes to this day, in spite of the religious nut jobs."

His horizons broadened, Manhart next reached out a helping hand to Vietnamese refugees who fled to the States in the aftermath of Saigon's fall and America's hasty retreat from that decimated country. He proudly remembers his involvement with one family's resettlement here:

"Somewhere in the '70s I was called and asked to find a sponsor for a desperate Vietnamese refugee family of six— Kang, Heng, and their two boys and two girls." Manhart said he tried enlisting his parish to aid them, but the pastor did not offer assistance and "the scared shitless parishioners" begged off as well. "So, Mary and I said we would sponsor them. I asked three buddies to 'lunch-and-loose' (as in loosen the purse strings) at the Omaha Press Club and conned them into helping out. Without a thought I am certain that the experience of this over several years was one of the most memorable and great things any of the eight of us ever had the opportunity to get into.

"The memories flood back and even the bad ones we can still laugh at without regret. The most obvious is our church really missed the showboat, especially the part when Kang had a few too many over dinner with me in the Old Market and told about his former business in Saigon. His bar there featured 'a bed of flowers'—comfort girls for the G.I.s. I had to make it very clear that he was not to relocate this former business here in Omaha. 'No flowers, Kang.'"

Manhart was finding that for himself, at least, he did not need to work within a religious institution in order to do the right thing or to carry out works of charity or to practice what Christ or Buddha or Muhammad preached. All he needed was the desire to take action and then to act. He was hardly alone in questioning church tenets and in breaking away to search for his own path to spiritual fulfillment and social justice.

In response to the changing times the Catholic church did open up in some areas. The more liberal attitudes were reflected in some Vatican II decrees that, while hardly radical, did foster a more humane, more grassroots liturgy and parish life that connected with people in real life ways. For example, the ancient Latin Mass was largely done away with in favor of Mass said in worshipers' native tongue. Instead of priests celebrating Mass with their back to the congregation, they began facing their congregants. The use of music during services was liberalized to allow guitars, drums, tambourines, and other instruments as well as contemporary songs to supplement the strict, traditional canon of religious music. Lay people were permitted to take on deacon roles that found them administering communion and reading scriptures during services and ministering to worshipers outside the church walls.

The church's efforts notwithstanding, Manhart found himself increasingly alienated from an institution that condemned or disapproved of many things he embraced. Instead of feeling that he broke with the church, he felt the church broke with him and like-minded folks who accepted racial, cultural, lifestyle, gender diversity and alternative points of view.

"Organized religion abandons people, it is not the other way around," he said. "I did not abandon Him\—God, I just realized God is probably a she." He said his own personal spiritual philosophy "came out of a lot of very difficult struggling." Instead of identifying himself with one religion or dogma or nationality, he has come to believe, as Gandhi did, that each of us is linked in an unbroken chain to humanity, plural, and our many beliefs, and therefore he takes the best from each on his journey of spirituality. By contrast, he said, almost any organized religion is "intolerant" of those espousing different affiliations and beliefs. That just does not square with Manhart and his Open Wide view of the world. That is another trait he got from his father and one he is glad to have inherited.

7

His Theatre Openings

The church was not immune to the spirit of revolution and renewal sweeping through the world. So it was that dance and other art forms were introduced into the Catholic liturgy. Outside of mass, parishes began taking a more proactive approach with parishioners, holding classes for prospective and already married partners, for divorced Catholics, for lapsed Catholics, for example. Amid all this reformation were familiar fund-raising events such as church festivals and bazaars and melodramas. Manhart was a member of St. Margaret Mary's Catholic Church when it staged a play as a benefit to support church operations. The ham in him could not resist trying out.

"In the '70s there was a play in our parish and they wanted somebody to play the villain. Well, [then–President Richard M.] Nixon was a hero/villain, so I played the villain. I was quite good at it and I started to act, then to direct. I figured you cannot even talk about sex, race, religion, or politics, so let's try theatre and pretend all of them," he said.

The die was cast. As deeply as he had thrown himself into the machinations of church, he next threw himself into the intricacies of the stage. First with parish melodramas, then his group Kingsmark II a few years later.

His true passion for the art form was clearly ignited at the Rudyard Norton Theatre, whose founder and namesake was a distinguished actor and director from the old school. An Omaha native, Norton grew up with Henry Fonda. The two cut their acting teeth in the early '20s at the Omaha Community Playhouse, which launched both of their careers. But whereas Fonda was that one in a thousand who went on to Broadway and Hollywood stardom, Norton remained a community theatre stalwart for whom acting was an avocation rather than the way he earned his living.

Joining a theatre company the way Manhart did with the Norton is like joining a family. It can be an all-encompassing experience, especially if you insinuate yourself in both the behind-the-scenes business of it and the on-stage performance aspect of it as Manhart did. "I got involved with the Norton Theatre when it was in the Old Market as both an actor and as a techie, and then I became the treasurer on their board. I found the place to move the Norton Theatre from downtown to Dundee [an old line, high rent neighborhood]. I negotiated that contract to help them get in there," he said.

The Norton originated in the back of a vintage building in the Old Market. He remembers it as "a tiny hole in the wall where you had to go from the outside back entrance around a hotel to get into the backstage."

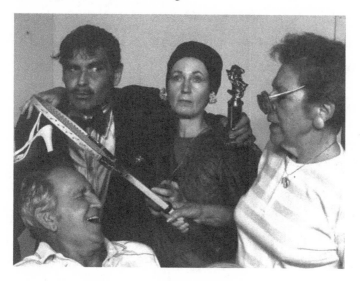

Some of the weird characters in *California Suite*.

Every thespian has anecdotes about the mishaps, near misses, and close calls that attend live performances, and Manhart is no exception. "Once," his story goes, "as the old fart in Moliere's *The Rivals*, I arrived an hour late since I was to make my house entrance in full period costume from the skin out to white face an hour into the show. Of course, because it was Sunday the curtain was an hour early. There was plump little director in the six-by-six lobby calmly waiting. She looked up at me over her glasses and said, 'Manhart, you have three minutes. We have written you out of the play.' By the time I had raced around the hotel to backstage, I was almost naked. I slammed on the layered costume, slapped on the white face and lavish wig, tore back to the lobby, scepter in hand, and made it down the center aisle for the best performance in my life. We all had our laughs, but it was not funny, and never have I been late since.

"That was a great time in my life. I started doing theatre in the '70s and I just kept doing more and more. The thing that really really convinced me about not only my ability on stage but about the importance of theatre was when I played Juliet's father in a Norton production of *Romeo and Juliet* that Dwayne Ibsen directed. I was forty-some-years-old then and that is the character I played—the forty-some-year-old Lord Capulet who has a fourteen-year-old daughter. Well, I had a fourteen-year-old daughter myself who had been in love. I had been through all that with her, and I used that experience in my portrayal. A patron who saw the show told me, 'I learned more than I ever did in psychology class! Now I understood how important theater is.'

"The other Norton production I played, *The Rivals*, is an absolutely hilarious play. I have always wanted to do that show again because it is as hilarious as any Neil Simon, but it is in the Restoration period," he said.

It was during this time he and Bonnie were first introduced to each other. Both were married at the time. It all began as a doctor-patient relationship before eventually evolving into a friendship over their shared love of theatre. It was after each divorced that they first dated. They likely would never have met, however, had she not had problems with her teeth and someone referred her to Manhart.

She recalled, "I met Mark in 1971 when my Greek neighbor told me, 'Go see this dentist before you have all of your teeth pulled.' I had a major issue with my teeth that took a lot of work. I did not have a lot of money, and so I became a subject to train Creighton dental students."

They did not know much about each other those first few years but enough to confirm they might share some mutual interests. "He knew I played piano a little bit and in the early '80s he asked me after one of my visits if I would put music to this show he was doing for Fr. Schwertley" (the same priest who compared Manhart to mercury).

Manhart was mounting plays for the Calix Society, a national support association for Catholic alcoholics, their friends, and loved ones, on behalf of Schwertley, a trained addiction counselor. Manhart recalled, "We would do this as a parish and they were so much fun. I asked Bonnie to adapt some music to a play. Schwertley did not know what to think of it but he let us do it. They said it would ruin the play. Well, the music made the play. Music is extremely important to almost any play and movie. We used to go around to cities around here putting it on." Bonnie ended up doing the music for a year.

Schwertley and Manhart go way back. They both attended Omaha Creighton Prep and Creighton University. Schwertley is a bit older than Manhart. After their school days they would bump into each other from time to time. When Manhart was still an adherent of organized religion and active in Catholic organizations, the two found themselves traveling in similar circles. Besides their shared Jesuit background and penchant for theatrics, they are also fellow Air Force veterans. But it was their mutual interest in creative pursuits that brought them together and keep them together to this day.

Schwertley remembers, "How I got connected with him more deeply was his show business inclinations. I was running a parish out in Fort Calhoun [Nebraska]. I liked doing skits and plays and stuff. I wrote them and acted in them. And I knew he was a good director and a good ham actor. He could play unusual roles because of his hawk-faced appearance. He ended up playing God in one play," said Schwertley. Those who feel Manhart has too high an opinion of himself would say that was typecasting.

Both men were also active in the Cursillo movement. The Christian, retreat-based spiritual program promotes the uniqueness, originality, and creativity of each person through the development of an empowering personal relationship with God. Reaching one's potential as an individual and in service to others is the aspirational goal of the program. It could describe the journey Manhart has been on his entire adult life.

Schwertley was the chaplain for the Omaha Cursillo chapter, and Manhart was its president. Through their shared spiritual interests the theatrical priest recruited the theatrical dentist to put on skits and plays for Calix. It was a match made in heaven, excuse the pun. Schwertley wrote and Manhart directed. They both acted. Cursillo held its national convention in Omaha in 1976, which was the occasion when Manhart played God.

As Schwertley noted, working in the close confines and intense manner that a play demands, theatre folks get to know each other in a short time. It is an intimate art. That's why after working with him a number of times he feels he has a pretty fair handle on Manhart, the man and the artist.

"I got to know him pretty well," Schwertley said. "He is an interesting character. He is hard to pin down. He is a very creative, avant-garde guy. He is an innovator. He is a maverick. But he is not one filled with hostilities, rather he is a colorful, likeable maverick. He is a very independent, outspoken guy, but he is not a hard guy to deal with. He will listen to you. He is a good man to talk to. He is a benevolent director. He does not bellow and holler at people, he keeps them at ease. He has the ability somehow to keep peace with nervous people."

That "ability to keep peace with nervous people" is a necessary skill in dentistry and in theatre, where patients, like cast and crew members, anxiously await the outcome. It gets back to why Manhart has the right temperament for doing what he does, the way he does it, which is offering calm, expert assurance to those putting their care and trust in his hands.

Schwertley's characterization of Manhart as being like mercury, as always squirting out some place new, could describe himself as well. For example, there is his life as a priest and then there is his creative or expressive life as a journalist, playwright, actor, and

bodybuilder. Schwertley got into weight training decades ago and still lifts today. He has written about physical fitness, as he has about addiction and spiritual matters. For years he wrote a column for the *Catholic Voice* newspaper, the publication that covers the Omaha Archdiocese. He worked as a reporter for several years before becoming a priest.

Manhart recalls that many years before weight training became standard practice in athletics, Fr. Jim recommended to the University of Nebraska football coaching staff that they adopt a strength program for their players to help improve on-the-field performance. The priest's recommendations fell on deaf ears then, but it was not long before UNL pioneered a strength and conditioning program that other college football programs liberally borrowed from.

Despite Manhart's caustic stances against the church and against authority, the two men remain friends. One suspects each sees himself in the other. If a priest can do theatre, why not a dentist? And vice versa. It turns out that Schwertley's father was an innovative physician. Way back in the 1930s his surgeon father advocated that post-operative patients get up and start moving as soon as possible in the hospital, "which was heresy at the time," said Schwertley, whose weight training practices and theatrical stagings certainly set him apart from the run-of-the-mill, doctrinaire priest.

That sounds an awful lot like the intrepid Manhart trait that found Paul Manhart picking up and leaving the farm for a law degree, stealing away his bride, Eleanor, to elope, and then throwing caution to the wind to tinker with this newfangled machine called a power lawnmower. Mark Manhart's own insatiable appetite for life and for taking an idea and running with it, no matter how far afield it seems from his core expertise, has been well established by now. It is what makes him endearing and fascinating.

Manhart's experience with the Norton and with the Calix plays led to his developing the Kingsmark II. He took the name from an old theatre company in Omaha. He and Bonnie were becoming thick as thieves by then in their shared theatre preoccupation. That is as far as it went they insist. Still, the two could hardly contain their enthusiasm, that is how regenerative the theatre was for them. An impetus for his next theatre incarnation, the Grande Olde Players, was a frustrating audition experience that he felt was a blatant example of ageism.

"A great newcomer fellow from Kansas City and I, both in our early forties, gave excellent auditions at the Omaha Community Playhouse as Atticus Finch for *To Kill a Mockingbird*, complete with a Southern accent, which Gregory Peck never really had in the movie classic," Manhart remembers. "We were both turned down for a twenty-five-year-old kid who would not know a black man, the law, or being the parent to two kids if they hung him with a used rope."

Whether or not Manhart and the actor from K.C. lost the part because of their age nobody will ever know, but there is no doubt that theatre, like film and television, has a history of casting younger people to play older roles.

Then, as Bonnie Gill remembered it, she and Manhart were at a coffee shop coming down from the high of a Calix performance when he broached the idea of the two of them starting a new theatre. The proposition took her by surprise. Bonnie knew that starting any new organization from scratch, much less getting it off the ground and running, is a tall order. Add to that it being a public-performance-based organization whose fortunes are tied to theatregoers' whims and one that is bound to perpetually struggle to generate enough revenue just to break even, and she had some idea of what she was getting herself into. Not to mention all the time it would take to run the business side, to market it, and, most time consuming of all, to mount productions—with many days and nights devoted to auditions, rehearsals, and performances.

If she was going to do it, it had better be a theatre with a distinct niche and mission that she could commit herself to body and soul. So, picking up on Manhart's recent frustration when he and that other middle-aged gent were denied a part, as he saw it, because they were too old, she told Manhart she would embark on a new theatre with him on one condition. " 'If you are going to do it,'" I told him, 'you have to do it with older people, to highlight their talents and capabilities.' That's because I was doing a journalism and gerontology degree at the University of Nebraska at Omaha. I did not have any spare time, I had kids and a business, and I had to make everything count," she said. In other words, it had to be a theatre she could apply her expertise to and that she could feel invested in. He loved the idea. And, so, as Manhart likes to tell it, the two of them conceived the Grande Olde Players over a cup of coffee.

They put up $750 to get the theatre off the ground.

Besides offering a rebuttal to the ageism both felt was rampant not only in theatre but in society at large, why did the idea of a theatre built on the talents of seniors appeal to them so? The mission or manifesto behind the Grande Olde Players really is a credo for the way Manhart and Gill see themselves and their lives as aging individuals. Thus, the theatre became a vehicle for dispelling myths that place artificial limits on the capabilities of people of a certain biological age without giving them a chance to show what they can do.

Through the theatre the couple and their cohorts advocated successful, active aging with every production they put on. Every performance demonstrated the efforts of vital seniors on stage and behind the scenes, each show loudly and clearly proving their point that seniors can do much more than be theatregoers, they can do theatre with the best of their younger counterparts.

James Thorson, former head of the UNO Department of Gerontology, where he still teaches, remembers that what began as a work-study experience for Gill turned into something much more. Before long, she ended up getting him involved, too. "Bonnie was one of our graduate students. Each of the students needed to do a practicum or field placement, working directly with older people as a supplement to their classroom studies. With the Grande Olde Players Bonnie got not only a practicum but also a husband. Not all of our practica were similarly successful. After a while, she started recruiting her professor to also be an actor, and I think I was in about a dozen plays over the course of the years," he recalled.

Bonnie said the Grande was well out in front of the curve in the 1980s in Omaha with its progressive stance on active aging before that concept became a popular lifestyle trend. It has now exploded into a giant industry catering to the growing senior population and the longer, healthier lives many are living.

"When Bonnie and I started the Grande Olde Players," Manhart said, "theatre folk really doubted the nutty idea of a couple with no formal theatre background, while the older people went nuts over it. Well, we put up a few hundred dollars apiece and made that back the first weekend of our first show, a one-act, *Any Body for Tea?*"

"Our very first show was a big hit," said Bonnie. "Steve Milsap with the *Omaha World-Herald* gave us a lot of praise. I remember saying, 'This is a gimme because older people already have that character.' So you did not have to do a lot of acting coaching. If you cast it right and you pick a fairly decent play, all you have to do is teach them how to project and not put their back to the audience."

That inaugural show was held at the Paxton Manor downtown, a former hotel converted into a senior living residence. Other borrowed spaces were used for performances, including Westminster Presbyterian Church. Soon, the theater found its own space.

The rest is history. "In 1984 we leased our own little building, in the former Golden Phoenix nightclub on 39th and Jones Streets, remodeled it into a theatre, stayed there five years. We were so successful we rented the place at 2339 North 90th Street in 1991, redesigned the space, and we ran that thing as a theatre for eighteen years," Manhart said with more than a hint of pride in the telling.

The Grande's play bill through the years included many classics, standards, and chestnuts from the American Theatre as well as quirky originals. The theatre's offerings decidedly ran toward the light but on occasion it was not afraid to take on more ambitious, difficult, serious material.

―――――――

Here is a sampling from select seasons:

2003–2004 Season

Solid Gold Cadillac by Teichman & Kaufman
The 1940s Radio Hour by Walton Jones
Hocus Pocus by Jack Popplewell
Gift of Murder by George Batso
Any Wednesday by Muriel Resnik
Ed Solomon Presents by Myrna Robbins

2002–2003 Season

Don't Drink the Water
    by Woody Allen Harvey by Mary Chase
An O. Henry Christmas by Peter Ekstrom
Spider's Web by Agatha Christie
Threepenny Opera by Kurt Weil
Return to Vaudeville by GOPT

2001–2002 Season

Wife Begins at 40 by Sultan/Barret/Cooney
Papa's Angels by Colin Wilcox-Paxton/Charles Jones
Angel Street by Patrick Hamilton
Everybody Loves Opal by John Patrick
You're a Good Man Charlie Brown by Clark Gesner
The 1940's Radio Hour by Walton Jones

2000–2001 Season

It Runs in the Family by Ray Cooney
Papa's Angels by Collin Wilcox-Paxton/Charles Jones
The Brides of March by John Chapman
Bone Chiller by Monk Ferris
The Silver Whistle by Robert McEnroe
I Do! I Do! by Schmidt and Jones

1996–1997 Season

A Bad Year for Tomatoes by John Patrick
The Importance of Being Uncle Roscoe? by Pat Cook
Unexpected Guest by Agatha Christie
Room Service by Murray and Boretz
Vaudeville Omaha '97 by GOPT

1994–1995 Season

Lost in Yonkers by Neil Simon
The Man Who Came to Dinner by Hart and Kaufman
Never Too Late by Sumner Arthur Long
The Matchmaker by Thornton Wilder
Vaudeville Omaha '95 by GOPT

1993–1994 Season

On Golden Pond by Ernest Thompson
On the Air by Donald-Brian Johnson
The Odd Couple by Neil Simon
Too Soon for Daisies by W. Dinner & W. Morum

1992–1993 Season

The Legend of Sleepy Hollow
   based on Washington Irving tale
Rumors by Neil Simon
Christmas in Vermont by Mark Manhart
The Hollow by Agatha Christie

1990–1991 Season

California Suite by Neil Simon
Pickwick's Holiday by Mark Manhart
Just Desserts by Pat Cook
A Candle on the Table by Patricia Clapp
Any Body for Tea? by C. B. Gilford
Yankee Doodle by Tim Kelly

Unusually well-outfitted for a small community theatre, the one-hundred-thirty-seat house featured an intimate stage, complete technical light and sound systems, dressing rooms, and storage areas. During the theatre's long run, the all-volunteer theater staff and board produced an average of five major shows a year, each with a dozen or more performances, and special events when the stage was dark, including a jazz concert series, puppet shows, storytelling, and cabaret.

The odds of any community theatre making it, then or now, are slim. Lasting more than twenty-four years as the Grande did is quite a feat because just during that span alone in Omaha many theatre companies came and went. Even in the best of times live theatre has a fairly limited audience. What customer-base there is has to be shared by Omaha's competing live theatres, by other performing arts, by movie theaters, et cetera. Just among stage theatres, the Grande had to contend with the Omaha Community Playhouse, the largest community theatre in the nation, as well as The Rose, one of the country's largest children's theatres. Then there's the opera, the symphony, the ballet, and so on.

With so many arts, entertainment, and leisure options available to people, a theatre must find a strong identity if it is going to separate itself from the pack and find a loyal following. That was the beauty and the genius of the Grande Olde Players—everything from the name to the people who staffed it to the performers on stage was a celebration and representation of the senior set.

"We were even criticized for having too many volunteers," Manhart recalls.

The theatre's unique niche and undeniable success caught the attention of producers at Nebraska Educational Television, who taped one of the Grande's shows before a live audience for airing on the statewide public television network.

Age was just a number at the Grande. No one was denied an opportunity because they were deemed too old. "We gave everybody a chance," Bonnie said. Still, she and Manhart were more than a little dubious of the capabilities of a quite elderly player in the theatre's first show. So unsure were they whether the late Lois Wayland could handle lines for the inaugural show, *Any Body for Tea?*, that the eighty-something woman was cast as a spinster who dies on page seven of the one-act play. But, as Bonnie tells it, "Until the end she remembered her lines. She came back six years later and did the lead in the three-act *Arsenic and Old Lace*. Lois and her seventyish co-star made up lines but they never got out of character." Lois remained a die-hard supporter of the theatre past her one-hundredth birthday.

Stories abound of people defying expectations at the theatre. Bob Ellsworth was retired when he realized a long-held dream of doing live theatre. Manhart said when he asked why he finally gave it a try, Ellsworth told him, "I am tired of playing cards and waiting to die." Theatre helped people blossom from shy mumblers into stentorian orators as they came out of their shells. "It is absolutely the most fun," Bonnie said.

Whereas the custom in theatre is for young actors to play old, the Grande reversed that tradition by having older actors play young. Sometimes it worked just fine and other times the age disparity stuck out like a sore thumb. It is not every older actor who can play much younger than his or her own years, especially when playing opposite a much younger person. Because many of the performers at the theatre were relative newcomers to the stage, and in some cases had never been on stage before, Manhart made the Grande a training ground for actors of all ages. He also helped develop directors.

The Grande earned a reputation for giving first-time directors a chance to direct shows and for giving second chances to theatre vets, most notably Charles Jones, who was let go by the Omaha Community Playhouse due to health problems. At the Grande he found a new home for his talent, "directing things he had always wanted to do," Bonnie said, "and never got a chance to do, like *The Three Penny Opera*."

Bonnie's own story mirrored that of many Grande Olde Players, as she overcame stage fright to act there and surprised herself by learning to direct. She and Manhart often co-wrote and directed shows.

Said Thorson, "Mark was great with his directors, giving them total support and creative freedom. As the founder of the theatre, he more or less acted as producer for the productions that he did not actually direct himself. As a director, he gave me perhaps too much freedom, as I would get bored after about the sixteenth performance and start adding or changing lines just to amuse myself. Cast as Mr. Paravacini in *The Mousetrap*, I was using what I thought was a credible Italian accent until I heard a tape recording of it. It was just awful, so I played the character with no accent at all, much to the mystification of the reviewer for the newspaper."

Beyond acting and directing, older folks found other niches at the theatre. Colene Moreno served as hostess/reservationist for twenty years and even after moving to an assisted living facility insisted on continuing in that role. Lew Ryan helped build sets, and he made the announcements at each show, warming up the audience with jokes. He donned a tuxedo for opening nights. Charlie Green and Jean Granlund hosted the theatre's opening night parties.

There was also a camaraderie that went beyond the normal fraternization of a theatre company and its patrons. "It was an intimate little theatre and it was almost like family," said Ryan. "I would be in the front lobby before the show and it got to the point I was on hugging terms with a very large percentage of the regulars."

8

His Faithful Dental Partner and Loyal, Satisfied Patients

When Manhart was not doing his church and theatre thing, he was attending to his practice. An adjunct professional activity that occupied much of his time for a period of years was teaching as an associate professor at Creighton University Dental School. One of his students in the late '60s and early '70s was Tom Steg, who is now his dental partner of thirty years. Steg paints a glowing picture of Manhart the teacher.

"He was very well liked. He is very good with students, he relates to students very well. He was one of the best instructors up there. He is very good at building a bond with his students and bringing out of his students a motivation to learn or an interest in what he is teaching," Steg said.

After graduating in 1973 Steg lost contact with Manhart for awhile as the younger man busied himself trying to establish his practice. He said, "I bought a practice in a little town called Hamburg, Iowa, which is about sixty miles south of Omaha, right on the Missouri border. I practiced there for about five years. One day I came across a patient who came in with endodontic problems. She had a broken front tooth, there was exposure of the nerve, and the inside of the tooth was not fully developed. From my experience with Dr. Manhart at Creighton, he talked about calcium and getting the apex to close on an undeveloped tooth. He had experience with that, I had not, so I called him up and referred that patient to him."

Steg began getting reacquainted with Manhart at dental meetings. There came a time when their shop talk and small talk turned to embarking on a potential business relationship. "Well, after about five years my wife kind of was disenchanted with small town life and wanted a bigger city like Omaha," Steg said. "At one of the dental meetings I mentioned to Dr. Manhart that we were thinking about moving to Omaha and he said, 'Why don't you come in with me?' And so I joined his practice in 1979."

Manhart had brought in previous dental partners to help in a variety of ways but none stuck around very long. Having someone to practice with, to bounce ideas off, appealed to him. "You do not want to practice alone, it's just lonely," said Manhart.

Neither man expected the partnership would last thirty-plus years and counting. In Manhart, Steg has found the perfect complement to himself. Where Manhart is a live-out-loud personality, Steg is a veritable wallflower. But they share in common an intense fascination with their profession and with pushing the limits of new therapies. There is a deep mutual respect.

"Everything just fit together, and we have never had to say anything or sign anything to make that work," said Manhart. "And practicing with him is so easy because I am doing things that are way off the wall as far as he is concerned and yet he has stayed here and he has listened and he has watched and he has contributed, and he is still doing this. He is there and he is supportive and we are both learning. I have discovered a couple things and he has discovered a couple things, and I do things he doesn't like sometimes and he does things I don't like, but it does not have anything to do with what is deep between us. And so we have been together thirty years. I think that is really unusual."

From Steg's standpoint Manhart is the ideal partner. "He is a very open-minded person. Some say he is eccentric. But where other people kind of have a locked view of things—this is how I was taught, this is how you do it, and there is no other way—he does not keep a closed mind to anything and is willing to try different things," said Steg.

That goes for Manhart's rich personal life as well. Steg said it is hard to wrap your arms entirely around all of Manhart because there is so much to him. "Most people find him kind of fascinating. I still do not have him figured out after all these years. Most people you can figure out, but he still baffles me."

One thing Steg is certain about is Manhart's character. "He is a very tolerant person. He looks at everybody the same way on an equal basis." He is also a generous man. Steg admires the fact that Manhart did a lot of pro bono dental work for the Vietnamese refugee community that settled in Nebraska. It is the kind of thing Manhart does with little fanfare, just like the humanitarian dental mission trip he made to Venezuela. More recently, he has worked with the indigent in Nebraska, donating care to the homeless.

Not long after joining Manhart, Steg became aware of his partner's explorations into new calcium therapies. "He was writing an article about doing root canals with calcium for submission to this esteemed dental journal, The Triple O or *Oral Surgery, Oral Medicine, Oral Pathology.* At the time I did not give him much of a chance of getting that article published, but he did, they published it. I mean, that is not easy to get in. Some journals are easier than others. Well, that one is a very difficult to get in. It was quite a triumph."

Then Steg began to observe some impressive treatment outcomes from Manhart's calcium therapies. "He had a patient who had an abscessed tooth and a fistula that was coming out of the side of the jaw. The abscess had gotten large in the bone and was looking for an escape. Pressure builds up and an infection often times will burrow out the side of the jaw and then start draining. Well, he was cleaning out that root canal and he got the idea to put some calcium in the root of the tooth to get the healing process started, and when he put that in, it went through the end of the root and out the fistula and came out the side of the jaw."

Both doctors were dumbfounded. Steg said, "He took a picture of it, he left it and had the patient come back in less than a week and that darn fistula had completely healed up. Amazingly." More amazing outcomes followed. "I think the biggest advancement is the one that led from the healing of the fistula. That led to the injection of the calcium materials underneath the gum so people do not develop deep pockets of periodontal disease, and in some cases placing even periodontal dressings over that to keep it in place and the dramatic healing that ensues. That was a major advancement because it eliminated the need for a lot of surgery."

Surgery is a dirty word to Steg and Manhart. They feel the need for much if not all periodontal surgery has been eliminated but are dismayed that it continues to be a somewhat routine recommendation. Steg agrees with Manhart that the periodontist's maxim of "to cut is to cure" has been too broadly accepted and applied. The partners believe surgery, which can be very expensive and require much after-care, not to mention the pain that it can induce, should only be used when all other options have been exhausted.

Besides, Steg said, "People have a fear of surgery and when they are told they need surgery and they hear how expensive it is, a lot of them will give up. It can lead to them feeling, 'Well, heck, I'm not going to do anything,' or 'I'm just going to have my teeth out.'" He believes that is a disservice to patients who could otherwise benefit from the kind of gentle and effective interventions that he and Manhart offer as alternatives to something as drastic as surgery.

"Our particular procedure for periodontal disease is painless, not expensive, works fast, helps people save their teeth. It is amazing," said Steg. "I had a patient here twenty some years ago. She had a pocket around her canine tooth. A dentist out in California had done a radical surgery cutting the gum back around that tooth. Years later I saw her and she had massive bone loss around that tooth and most any dentist would have removed it. Well, I started treating it with the calcium materials, and twenty years later she still has the tooth and it is absolutely amazing."

Those kinds of results served as the impetus to keep moving forward. "That really instigated finding out about the healing properties of calcium," Steg said. "It was a moment that kind of led to all the treatments in periodontal disease." It is precisely how the pair still operate today. In classic scientific method mode, the two men float ideas, scrutinize them, discard some, test others. It is theorizing, experimentation, trial and error at a very grassroots, practical level.

Steg described how they work out solutions: "We have a lot of conversations and feed things back and forth, trying to help both of us come up with new ideas, such as one of the things we are doing with root canals. We are still in the process of doing it. There is a little point made of paper we put in there to dry the tooth out. We kibitzed back and forth and came up with coating the thin paper points with calcium powder and then using them to dry the canals. This would deposit slight amounts of calcium throughout the inside of the tooth, which would not only dry but disinfect the canals."

Formulating the products their Calcium Therapy Institute makes, markets, and sells is a collaborative process as well. Manhart arrives at the exact compounds after consulting with Steg. "Tom has helped enormously just by the two of us talking and figuring it out, and we make it right here," said Manhart. "It started as a lark. So many people were

inquiring about calcium materials, we said, why don't we send the people who are making inquiries something they can try at home, on a modest scale, for minor problems? We thought that then maybe that will encourage them to think maybe this idiot has got something to say and then eventually they will come in and have their teeth worked on."

That is precisely what has happened with hundreds of patients. One afternoon Manhart sifted through a pile of correspondence on his desk to produce a letter from a woman in Germany whose handwritten communication helped him to make his point.

"She went to eight dentists all over Germany and got the same story. Sixty thousand marks to save her teeth. After she found us on the Web, she and her husband came here. We got her teeth in good shape for a few thousand dollars and we sent her home with materials. She tried them and now she orders materials once in a while to maintain her teeth," Manhart said.

That story has been repeated many times with other patients—some as far away as El Salvador, Great Britain, and France. So much so, Manhart said, that "it has turned into a mail order business all its own for products like the toothbrush, the rinse, the skin lotion, the chips. We have people we have seen in the office, like the lady in Germany and a couple from England, who we send the calcium materials to in order for them to do the follow-up treatment at home. Some months we probably now send out a hundred self-care kits compared to maybe one a month when we started. There are a few larger orders. I even have agents now who are starting to sell them around the country."

Another aspect of his practice Manhart takes pride in is how he resolves problems in patients whose dental problems have been deemed hopeless and for whom the only recommended solution by other dentists was the complete removal of their teeth.

"We have handled the most hopeless cases you can think of," he said. "The lady from Germany had been to eight or ten dentists all over Germany, and they all wanted to take her teeth out. We have treated her two or three times, sent her materials to use, and she has a little trouble every once in a while but she has not lost a single tooth. Patients come in where you have to hold the teeth down in order to clean them. That is how loose they are. Literally, if you did not hold them, the cleaning process would pull them out. We treat them, and we let the body decide how many teeth it needs to get rid of. We may have to take one or two out.

"I have patients I started thirty-five years ago that way, and they have not lost three teeth, five teeth all these years. The healing process occurs so rapidly it is just incredible, and so it becomes a magic thing to these patients. They just do not believe the difference we make," he said.

Satisfied patients abound. Just a sampling of testimonials received by the Calcium Therapy Institute from patients, including dentists who have either been treated themselves or have completed calcium therapy treatment training, follows:

"Smile more, eat better, sleep better. Thanks so much for the toothbrushes. Before (the calcium therapy) treatment I had hardly been able to really smile for some time. I can smile now! Not only that, but I can eat now and food tastes better. Also, my mouth tastes better. And I can actually eat anything now. I used to avoid all kinds of foods. I can drink cold water now. I sleep better because I can eat real food now and I have no more pain. My teeth are stronger. I'm really, really happy with all you have done for me. No one has ever scratched the surface of all you have done for me in just one visit. I am bringing my

daughter out with me because she was so impressed with what you did for me."

—Kathy in Santa Barbara, Cal.

"I cannot tell you how happy I am that I made the trip to Nebraska for treatment. I feel for the first time that I actually got answers, and having you probe for the cause so diligently did my heart (and gums) great good."

—Antoine in California

"Thank you for your wisdom, diagnosis and care of my teeth. Thank you for sending out the new kit. My bite still feels good and the dressings are still in place. I remember the things you told me and I know that it was all excellent advice. I like your conservative philosophy. I'll be in touch. I appreciate your care and concern."

—Joan in Missouri

"The self-care treatment program offered some relief and improvement, but nothing compared to the result of my ultimate visit to Omaha, where two treatments have resulted in a vast improvement."

—Martin in Scotland

"As for me and my interest, I'm a woman who was diagnosed in 1993 with periodontal disease. Two dentists, a periodontist, and a facial surgeon have been my companions on a journey I couldn't recommend to anyone. I found Manhart ... and have flown six times to visit him in Omaha. The results have been

more than I could have hoped for or thought possible. You see, the impressions had already been made for a full denture (for me) and as of today I still have my own teeth and the impressions for a denture are still sitting on a shelf where I am desperate for them to stay."

—Debra in Ohio

"My story, very briefly, is that I had orthodontic treatment done late in life which did not resolve itself. I had it investigated and was told by a top UK oral surgeon that I would lose all my teeth since I had advanced periodontal disease. I went on the Net, found Dr. Manhart, considered the alternatives in the UK and USA, got an expensive opinion from the top periodontist in the UK and, after about a year of emails to the Calcium Institute, decided this was the only road I wanted to take. My condition was fairly advanced and complex as I was still wearing a retainer to keep my front teeth in place. My visit was the best thing I have ever done for my teeth. I cannot commend him enough to you, both for his pioneering periodontal work and also his dental expertise generally."

—Linda in England

"Doc, I feel like I have my own teeth back. My gums have never felt so good. I'll talk with anyone you like about how it's a miracle for me. And now I don't get that tartar on my teeth, even on the front ones."

—Vern in Nebraska

"*Doctor, everything is fine. I can really feel a difference in the way my teeth fit together! Everything you told me made perfect sense and I cannot believe that I had no pain. I wish I had known about this four years ago.*"

—Kyra in Missouri

"*I would like to tell you how pleased I am with the wonderful progress I have made in restoring health to my gums and teeth since using your products. I have hardly any plaque buildup on them, my gums have tightened up, and I had a loose tooth which has no movement at all any more. As a matter of fact my dentist at one point wanted to do a root canal (which I refused) on a tooth which I still have and does not give me any trouble at all any more. I am sure thats thanks to you ... I will be able to keep all the teeth I have. Another thing I have noticed is that the white color is returning slowly instead of having that opaque look to them, another bonus I was not expecting. I even look forward to brushing my teeth knowing how good my gums feel after and how silky my teeth feel for hours and that they are just getting healthier all the time. The only regret I have is that I had not discovered your system before I started having trouble ... I am sharing my products with people that need them badly and can hardly wait to see their improvement as I did.*"

—Sharon in Calgary, Canada

"I keep one (a Calcium/Zinc Toothbrush) next to my keyboard, where I spend most of my days. When I feel like a cigarette, I just brush my teeth with the toothbrush. Your brush has caused me to smoke less."

—Franklin in California

"I received my toothbrushes (since an office treatment) and I think they really help. My mouth feels clean afterward, not antiseptically clean, but naturally clean. So, thank you. .... mmmmm."

—Joan in Missouri

"I like how my mouth feels after using the Calcium/Zinc Toothbrush! My teeth feel really clean, and my gums feel great! Completely different from using [popular brands of toothpaste], etc.!"

—Fay in California

"Thank you for sending the calcium treatment (Self-Care Kit) you sent me. It has improved my gum condition quite a bit. I told others about it too and hope that they contact you soon."

—Maryland

"Thanks so much for your help. The chips have relieved my pain after three uses. I will be getting in touch with you to order more when my supply gets low. You are a lifesaver!"

—Vickie in Florida

"I ordered the Self-Care Kit and am quite pleased. My local dentist said I needed gum surgery. After using your products for three months, she [the dentist] said it was no longer necessary."
—Carl in South Carolina

"Dear Doctor, thanks so much for taking care of this. I really appreciate it! I just don't want to run out of these products because they are WONDERFUL! I have been experiencing great benefits from them. I have been telling my friends and co-workers about calcium therapy and encouraging them to check out the website. I am so grateful for calcium therapy!"
—Judy in California

"Thanks once again for the brushes. I also want to thank you for the sample of calcium skin cream. I used it on a very dry patch of skin on my neck (I have no idea why I had it) ... and within a few days the dry skin was gone. I had tried several other lotions, etc., to get rid of this and nothing worked. I was nicely surprised that the calcium skin cream did the trick."
—Sam

"I have had acne since I was thirteen and in two weeks using the skin cream, I can't believe how it's gone and feels great. Send more!"
—Kevin in New York

"This is the most exciting thing I've learned in new dentistry since graduating eighteen years ago."

–A dentist trained by CTI
to perform the calcium therapy in Iowa

"Learning the calcium therapy turned me around one hundred eighty degrees about periodontal treatment. It works beautifully."

—A dentist in California

"[Since learning of the calcium therapy] we have started treatment on conditions considered 'hopeless' by other dentists. I'm amazed and impressed with our results already."

—A dentist from New England

"I have spent about twenty-five years trying to find a way to treat my periodontal patients without hurting them. Then you waltz in here, with all the answers, and you have been doing this for forty years? This is amazing."

—A dentist in Arizona after a short lecture
and some time in Manhart's office with a patient

Resolving dental problems is a true collaborative process at the Calcium Therapy Institute known as CTI. Steg finds great satisfaction in the invigorating banter and brainstorming he and Manhart engage in to determine the best course of action or the best solution.

"That is how new ideas come forth. I suppose he is more the scientific-type mind where he will probe and probe in brain sessions to try and come up with something new. That is what it takes," said Steg. "He is not afraid to try something new. He is a very stimulative person and I need stimulation. I practiced alone five years before I joined him and I was frustrated not having someone there to talk things over with, to get other ideas. I enjoy that because no one has all the answers themselves, and of course with Dr. Manhart he is out of the box, he has all kinds of ideas, and that is how advancements are made."

That kind of from-one-craftsman-to-another discussion, Steg said, is valuable "in the general practice of dentistry. Say you have a patient who is having a particular problem, well you can sound out your partner on it, and he may have a different perspective on it and go, 'Why don't you try this?' or 'Why don't you try that?' and it might be something you never thought of." He said Manhart sometimes has too many ideas for his own good. "Sometimes they are too far-fetched and it is a dead end, but you don't know unless you pursue."

Steg must be especially alert to keep up with Manhart, whose creativity and eloquence set a high bar. "He is more imaginative than I am. He is very good with words. He is a good writer. He searches for the right word. Things have to be worded properly. He is very well read. So he is an interesting person to talk to."

Manhart appreciates having Steg as his checks and balance confidante and advisor when it comes to getting to the bottom of a dental conundrum. "It is really good to practice with Dr.

Steg because he will see it and say, 'Hey, wait a minute, you are not quite right there.' He is brilliant and he is honest and he does not need to market his patients. He just touches them and they won't go anywhere else."

Both men are convinced that neither of them would have developed as much in their profession if they had practiced alone or apart these past thirty years. Each has pushed and prodded the other to new heights that would have been unthinkable in isolation. Similarly, they are sure that the work of the Calcium Therapy Institute would not be as far along as it is today without the collegial interplay that distinguishes their relationship.

9

Shots: This May Sting a Little, Ouch

It is no surprise to Mark Manhart's dental partner Tom Steg that Manhart has elicited the enmity of specialists, particularly periodontists, who have generally had the field of treating gum disease to themselves for a long time.

"A lot of dentists do not enjoy periodontal-type work," explained Steg. "They would rather just be doing crowns or bridges or partials than going through the process of getting somebody's gums in good shape." Manhart's willingness as a general practitioner to do periodontal work puts him out of step to begin with. The fact he decries the surgical approaches employed by periodontists makes him an antagonist in their eyes. Anything that threatens the periodontist's anointed realm, such as the calcium therapies, is met with contempt or worse, at least that is the way Steg and Manhart perceive it.

Manhart does not mince words when it comes to his nemesis, the periodontists. Where they claim he is practicing outside his field of expertise and thus infringing on their domain, he alleges the need for periodontal work as a specialty has been made defunct by his therapies. Where some specialists harangue him for not giving away his findings for free, he counters that these high-earning doctors are more than capable of affording the ordinary, conventional professional service fees he charges for training and, what is more, that he is entitled to be compensated for his own discoveries. These discoveries amount to his own products of the kind that have real commercial value. Where they say he is a fringe practitioner, he says these specialists are the ones who are on their way out once calcium therapies become the standard for care.

"We do not need you, we have not needed you for forty years," he tells periodontists. "We do not need hygienists anymore because what we do eliminates their job. Now if you want to continue doing what you are doing, that's fine, but if you want to learn this new way, we would be very happy to teach it to you; we don't care who you are, it's just that you have got to pay for it, just like everybody else paid for it. Nobody owes you information, nobody owes you any kind of professional expertise."

He does not like the fact that periodontists have come to call certain procedures by the terms *deep cleaning* or *scaling* or *root planing,* when in actuality gum surgery is being performed. These procedures, he said, are time intensive, uncomfortable, and costly.

"If you did it gently and quickly and without anesthesia and did not hurt the patient, that would be fine, and if you had something to use beforehand to help get ready for that, like the calcium treatment, and after that, to help soothe everything you have done, and if it would only take five minutes and the patient would be feeling great, then I would accept that, and we do that all the time in our practices. We just call it cleaning and calcium treatment," he said.

But he said the reality is that patients are "in agony for a week, two weeks after traditional gum surgery. The rule is, you have periodontal surgery and then you have dressings on your teeth for ten to twelve days, and I have had my friends and my family who have had that done [by other dentists], and they do not want to talk about it with me, it was so bad. When you cannot even eat a week later, when you cannot even chew a week later, I mean, my God ... I have had a patient come to me a month, two weeks after a deep scaling and they are still in agony and you treat them with these calcium materials and in ten minutes they feel wonderful. What we have is something that can be done with the cleaning and scaling with no anesthesia, and we can use the calcium materials before we even start cleaning, right when we are cleaning and afterwards, and it is very, very easy to do. The cost is very reasonable and the effectiveness just blows the whole hell out of the concept of hygiene."

A regular schedule of calcium applications, he said, has great palliative effects. "We have learned in the last several years that once you find the underlying causes and follow that routine for three months or six months, which is not a long time, you have solved their periodontal problem, even the cystic problem up in the front. What happens is very clear. They come back in after six months or eight months and there is virtually nothing to clean. And when you start seeing that over and over and over again in your practice, you have to say to yourself, we have resolved *the* most problematic things in dentistry, and so instead of seeing that patient year after year doing all kinds of dental work, their need for dental care goes way down."

He said this measured approach to dentistry flies in the face of the radical approach that has become predominant. "Organized dentistry pretends to be innocent as if our profession should do as much dental care as we can on people, rape them quickly, and get our money out of it. Well, the more that is done, the more surgery that is done, the more cosmetic dentistry that's done, the faster people lose their teeth, and the faster people lose their teeth, the less work there is to do because people with dentures do not need any work. I mean, is that very dumb or is that dumber than dumb?"

He said his calcium therapies could be easily adopted by any dental office and, furthermore, that hygienists could be easily trained to do much of the work.

"We could take almost 90 percent of the calcium therapy approach to the whole practice of dentistry and put it in the hands of the hygienist without changing even one regulation or one law in the whole profession," he said. "And who would be the heroes? The hygienists would be the heroes, the dentists would be the heroes, and the specialists would be the heroes. Applications of the calcium materials are related to every single one of our specialties, and there are so many aspects that need research right now. We have done a little bit of research, and every time we have done it, we have come up with great results," he said.

"We figure if we had had that normal, everyday kind of connection between scientists and professionals and research and clinical practice starting in the '60s, periodontal disease would not exist in this country as of twenty years ago and by this time would not exist in the world, and that is like saying we would have solved one of the most common diseases of humankind," he speculates.

Viewed in these terms, he said the de facto suppression of his findings is not so much his loss as the loss of countless millions of people who could be enjoying the fruits of dentistry's labor. One of the ways that organized dentistry has effectively kept a lid on his work and has marginalized it, he said, is through intimidation. The periodontal and

221

endondontic blocs in dentistry are strong, and specialists from these groups have found various ways to make Manhart aware in no uncertain terms that they do not want his work propagated.

"Periodontists tend to scare people about lawsuits," said Tom Steg. "A periodontist may tell you, 'Oh, if you do not diagnose that person's periodontal condition, you may be subject to a lawsuit. You have to send them to me so I can heal that; otherwise you are going to get sued.' If a legal case does ensue, a periodontist may even testify in court that a patient had some periodontal disease and such-and-such a dentist did not diagnose it or inform the patient of it, and as a result a lot of dentists are afraid to treat periodontal disease.

"Of course it is a good money-making thing for the periodontists," Steg went on, "who charge many thousands of dollars [per procedure]. If you are doing something that takes business from them and hurts their pocketbook, they are not going to be for it."

Manhart has been roundly criticized by specialists who believe he is out of his depth and out of bounds in using and advocating the use of calcium materials for periodontal issues. When he is on the receiving end of an attack, he gives it back as good as he gets it.

"I was down in Kansas City [Missouri] talking to a group of thirty dentists, and a specialist got up in the back of the room and said, 'You cannot do this, you have to start all over, you have to go back and do your lab studies, you have to do your animal studies, then your human studies, then we will consider whether you can do this or not.' And I said, 'No, I won't stop, I can't stop, I have been doing it for fifteen years and that is not the way science works anyway.' I said, 'Science works this way: some researchers do the lab studies in South America, some other researchers do the animal studies in England, and someone like me does the human studies in the United States, and all of that is happening at the same time," Manhart told his colleagues.

"It is global think is what it is and that is the way all medicine works, and all business works. And then what really got the periodontist pissed was, I said, 'What you are really asking me to do is to stop doing what we are doing, and stop progressing and learning, so that you can catch up and put your name on it,' and the specialist sat down, silent."

THE LAWS AND THE ORTHODOX

In the 1980s Manhart learned first-hand just how far some orthodox specialists were prepared to go in defending their turf from him, someone they viewed as an interloper, a poacher, a dilettante, a critic, a crackpot.

"I did a lot of endodontics," he said. "I was promoting nonsurgical root canal therapy with calcium materials. All at once I get this lawsuit filed against me for misrepresenting or malpractice on this patient that I had seen. The patient had been to another dentist. Someone got this young, not too brilliant attorney to help this patient sue me and the case was presented against me."

The case was heard in an Omaha district court. "They said in court they were going to bring specialists in to testify against me and just by sheer coincidence I had a patient that had come to me not long before who I treated for a root canal that had failed. Surgical endodontics—surgical root canal therapy—had been done by a specialist, and we treated this patient nonsurgically with calcium materials and solved the problem. So I did what any professional would normally do. I dropped a note to the specialist who did the surgical root canal, saying that his patient had been to see me and things worked out really great with the patient and thank you very much for being part of this whole treatment," he said.

"After that no root canal specialist would testify against me and the reason is very simple. In my estimation he had screwed up," Manhart said. "We had fixed it, and things were right for the patient and nothing else need be said about that except that I used the calcium therapy to tell him everything is okay despite the fact that you screwed up. And that is all the further that it ever went because the root canal specialists realized if they testified against me, they would very quickly be answering questions about their own work and whether they were practicing legitimate root canal therapy and not whether I was."

Eliminating some specialists from the witness stand was not enough to deter the attorney for the plaintiffs, who lined up a number of others to lambaste Manhart. "When my neck was out there on the chopping block, there were several periodontal specialists who came in to testify against me. These were my friends and colleagues testifying against me, that is, the head of the periodontal department at the University of Nebraska, the people that were doing periodontal work in Omaha, and the gurus of periodontal therapy in this whole region. However, the oldest, most experienced one in Omaha did not and I never knew why."

From Manhart's perspective, this overkill of expert witnesses all mouthing variations of the same old groundless objections sounded awfully familiar. "They said that what I had done with this patient was unprofessional, that calcium therapy was not a treatment accepted in this area, that as my counterparts they did not agree with this and would not treat their own patients this way, and therefore it cannot be condoned. Another example they tried to use against me was I had built a bridge for a patient, and they said I should not have built the bridge because the teeth were not ready for it. Their contention was the teeth were not strong enough. It is all subjective though. I countered, 'Were you there? Did you feel how strong it was, did you sense the real condition?'"

He found himself butting heads with the old guard and its rigid rules and outmoded notions.

"There is a rule that is still very strong in dentistry and it is this: We cannot treat you, we cannot do things like restore crowns or bridges until your periodontal problem is solved. Well, when we were developing this whole concept of this approach of using calcium materials, there is a lot more to it than simply applying calcium to the mouth, to the teeth. There are other aspects to it," Manhart said, "like, are the teeth strong enough to start restoring? Is the bite correct? Does the dental work in your bite fit you or does it have to be adjusted? What can we do to help you resolve the stress in your bite, especially about the stress of your teeth and jaw? These are really critical things that cause stress in the mouth and in a patient's life.

"You can destroy a person's mouth by telling them they need all their teeth out, you have to have implants, you have to have surgery, it is going to cost you thousands of dollars up front, and then we cannot guarantee that work for more than three to five years."

The objection to calcium treatments, he said, boiled down to no more than "this idea of whether it was accepted by my peers. Well, that is an old, old concept in legal matters. Today, it is much more like, would you do this on another human being?" He said under direct questioning by his attorney the specialists' arguments were exposed for what they were—feeble, uninformed, prejudicial attempts at character assassination.

"They were asked things like, 'Do you know anything about this treatment? Have you ever done this?' They answered,

'No.' My attorney said, 'Dr, Manhart's been doing this for years, he has published papers on it and just a couple years ago he published an article on it in the international dental journal, The Triple O, so this information has been available. Have you read it? Do you understand it?' Their answers: 'Well, I'm not sure,' or 'It's no good so I don't read it.' They dismissed it because the local universities here did not teach it," Manhart related.

The whole imbroglio cast into relief for Manhart some bigger questions in his mind of how dental progress is impeded by special interests. Manhart indignantly asks his self-righteous critics, do you mean to say a treatment does not exist unless you decide it exists? How does basic science work? How are things discovered and how do they become popular or in this instance treatment of choice? He said treatment of choice means what treatment would be the best one to use in this instance and whether or not that is a generally accepted idea or practice, and whether or not more choose that than some other treatment. In other words, is this an accepted treatment by your peers in this era? He said that is all well and good but it does not hold water legally.

"Courts have come out and said in a sense that is nice but it's not enough to make a legal challenge to anything rational or humane, so they place it in the framework of is this something you would do to your fellow human being; namely, if this treatment is so good, is it the kind of thing you would do on your wife or on a colleague? That issue has not been confronted as much as the old answer to the issue—is this something your fellow dentists would do? Because your fellow dentists could be just as wrong or just as right as you are, and so that is not enough to justify a judgment about the issue," Manhart argues.

"Nowadays if a dentist is confronted before the court with this issue—should I do periodontal or root canal therapy in this way?—then you have to answer—is this something I would do on my peers? And then most of the time the answer comes out much different, especially in terms of something like periodontal surgery because, you see, there are many things in my field I see dentists do that they would never do on their loved ones or friends," he said.

An example Manhart finds instructive on this point is a call he took from a dentist in Colorado who wanted to bring his wife in to have a calcium treatment done to address her periodontal problems. Manhart said he asked the dentist why he would not just have his wife treated by a peer periodontist in Colorado. It did not take Manhart long to find out that this dentist "knew better. He knew how terrible it is, he knew the real implications of the whole surgical process, and the long recovery period and the likelihood of it working for only three to five years."

Manhart said, "The dentist did not want to subject his wife to all that. And so I said, 'If she would come in, I would treat her like any other patient,' and the Colorado dentist insisted that he be there and learn how to do it. I said, 'Well, I would not be treating you would I?' 'Oh, no, but if I had my name on it, I could sell it all over Colorado.' In other words, what he was doing was using his wife to learn what we knew about this therapy, the calcium therapy, with Dr. so-and-so on it, that we have struggled all our careers to develop. He wanted to come in on the shoulders of his wife, using her diseased condition as a way of learning what he would normally pay thousands of dollars to learn if he were coming as someone we train."

"Well, I am sorry," Manhart told him, "but you pay for education, you do not get it free because you are a dentist and because your wife needs treatment. The same way you do not learn radiology by having your wife's X-rays taken while the radiologist teaches you that specialty."

Any inclination Manhart harbored to let bygones-be-bygones with the lawsuit filed against him faded when his attorney discovered and squelched an attempt by the plaintiffs to enter Manhart's recent divorce record into the proceedings.

"That really did it for me with these guys," he said. The whole ugly episode of a court case should never have happened, but the special interests wanted to send a message. Instead of discrediting him, however, they discredited themselves.

"My attorney would just make them look like, Don't you specialists know anything? What are you saying here? This is bullshit. One guy came down two or three times and was paid like hundreds of dollars to testify against me, and he got up on the stand and he not only made a fool of himself once, but he made a fool of himself again. It got so embarrassing the judge and jury would laugh at these guys. I began to really feel embarrassed I was even known as a dentist because these people were so unprofessional, so childish, and so literally dumb," Manhart said.

"My attorney had told me, 'These guys are out to get your license, that is all they want, they do not care about this patient, they do not care about root canal therapy, they are out to get your license,' and that became an apparent situation. It was just so obvious."

Manhart was not taking any of it lying down without a fight. A Midwest-based dentist he had trained in calcium therapy and who used it in his own practice came to testify on his behalf. "He was a very professional person, a very knowledgeable witness to what I was doing," said Manhart.

In the end Manhart prevailed in what proved to be a nuisance lawsuit. "When the jury went out to deliberate, it only took them about thirty minutes to decide in my favor," he said. "It was immediately appealed to the Supreme Court in Lincoln and the judge would not even address it."

Bonnie Gill was in his life at the time of the trial but the two were not yet married. She sat in the courtroom during the proceedings, offering support. She recalled the relief they felt when the verdict was read.

She said, "The thing I always remember about that is the jury in a half hour acquitted him. It was so obvious that it was a set-up and yet those dentists turned around and went to the Nebraska Supreme Court, which meant he was on probation for two years. I mean, he practiced but he had to be very careful."

As a defendant whose competence was being called into question, Manhart was fortunate to have had good representation. "His attorney was absolutely fantastic," said Bonnie. "She told us point blank, 'It is a conspiracy, I would bet my life on it.' She said we could turn around and sue the dentists who made baseless claims against him, because think about what their allegations did to Mark's reputation and how many patients he lost, but she advised us not to. She said, 'I want you to know we could get through with the whole thing and win and the judge could ask for a dollar for everything we brought up in this suit, and I can tell you by looking at his face right now he is not going to do it.'"

Sensing how deeply this had wounded him, Bonnie said she is sure Manhart "wanted to [pursue a civil suit], he just wanted that revenge," but in the end he followed his attorney's advice and decided to let it go. Still, Bonnie said she did not fully appreciate just how hurt Manhart had been by the concerted effort to defame him and just how elaborate and real that effort was until an encounter at the Grande Olde Players.

She told the story, "I thought he was so confirmed by his suspicions when one night Dr. Ben Lynch, who used to be the dean of Mark's dental school at Creighton, came to the theatre and he said to Mark during intermission, 'Manhart, I do not know how you made a living all these years in Omaha with what all we have done to you.' He told Mark the real story and included himself in the whole lousy mess. It was his way of apologizing for being in it. That was good for me to hear because I live with this and sometimes I think, oh, you are full of it, Mark. You know, I do not know how much is paranoia and how much is real."

Rather than get angry or smug about Lynch's disclosure that there had been a concerted effort mounted by the organized dentistry gang and that Lynch was complicit in it, Manhart appreciated his colleague's "confession." He always admired Lynch. The older man was one of those veteran practitioners he looked up to. According to Manhart, Lynch came right out and told him, "We spent thirty years here trying to stop you." The fact he said "we" was very important. That admission answered every question Manhart had.

Lynch also made it clear that the same organized dentistry gang did what it could to make Manhart persona non grata within local dental circles. "I never got the feeling he was remorseful," Manhart remembers. "Ashamed perhaps. He was very adult about it by saying in essence, yeah, it was us that did it. He was taking ownership of what he was involved with."

Lynch's coming clean with his conscience left Manhart with some deliberation of his own. "It made me think, what does a young guy do about those kinds of things? What do you do? You have got a choice of getting very pissed off, which I did, and staying pissed off and ruining your own self, or trying to keep putting it behind you. My thinking came around to just try to get through it. Don't forget it, but don't let it stop you from trying to accomplish what you are trying to accomplish."

Manhart knows all too well what it is like to become disenchanted and to feel one's ideals or principles betrayed. It is why he despairs what may happen to other dentists who come up against the wall.

"As an educator—and I consider myself an educator whether I am teaching at a school or not—I think to myself, what do I tell a young person like Bonnie's daughter that is going to keep her being a dentist for the next thirty years? What is going to prevent her from getting the hell out like a lot of dentists do? A lot of dentists make a lot of money and they are there to make a lot of money fast so they can get the hell out," he wondered.

"Because I cannot tell young dentists to go learn a lot at dental school and stick with organized dentistry. I cannot tell them that anymore, and I cannot tell them that if you discover something wonderful to go and try and tell everyone about it. Instead, I would have to tell them if you develop something that is really important, do not try and talk to your fellow American dentists, you are wasting your time, like I wasted years trying to. No, I would tell them, go to Europe, go to Asia. To me that is especially true because

Europe, India, and China are on the cutting edge of a lot of things, including dentistry," he would advise.

The experience of hearing Lynch confirm what Manhart always alleged was a conspiracy against him, combined with the smear campaign of the lawsuit, helped Bonnie come to terms with some things. For one, she said she came to understand that sometimes paranoia is justified because there really is someone out to get you.

"There is no question," she said, "one thing I learned in that trial that blew me away was I watched people who were destroying him get on the stand and act like there was nothing wrong, and I knew that was not their normal behavior. Or they were on the stand destroying him and when they were on the outside someplace, they were saying just the opposite. And it was like, Holy Toledo, how can you deal with this? Who can you believe?"

For this biography Manhart was asked if he would be willing to go through the court transcripts to flesh out some details but he declined, stating, "No, don't ask me to go looking for things in it because it is just too painful. It tore my life apart and I have no interest in getting into it again." Indeed, why relive a trauma for no good reason? He said his divorce, the court case, the theft of his patent—"that all happened in a short period of time in my life and I am not interested in dwelling on it because there are too damn many things that have happened."

ASSOCIATED TRAUMAS

Bonnie attests to the trauma the trial caused her mate on top of other traumas that befell him around the same time. "When we got together, he had had in 1983 and 1984, somewhere in there, a major heart attack in Denver when he was with his kids skiing. He was hospitalized a long time."

He tells the story, "I was on a ski slope in Colorado and it was too much, it was too high, and I had to be hauled out on a helicopter, and I spent time in the hospital there and then I came home." He underwent complicated heart surgery in later years. To this day, he said, "The sound of a helicopter bothers me, and I hate to go to hospitals, even to visit someone."

It was not his first brush with death. "It is a familiar place," he said of the precipice that is the near-death experience. Shortly after his honorable discharge from the Air Force he survived an accident in the Yukon that nearly totaled the car he was driving with two passengers in it, including one of his brothers. Packed to the gills, the weight unevenly distributed, the third fellow lost control of the car on a narrow winding road and the vehicle went careening off the highway and down the mountain slope, rolling several times before somehow ending up on the wheels. "That is pretty damn lucky," Manhart said.

He does not like to make a big deal out of skirting death. "Number one, it is nobody else's business. Not to be nosing into my life, but who in the hell cares? You know, is it that important? I doubt it, I really doubt it. It is important to me. But to the next ant on the hill, who cares? And it is very self-serving."

If those experiences were not enough, Manhart then went through his divorce and the lawsuit and trial, the stress of which nearly did him in again.

"When we were at trial, I really thought we were going to lose him," said Bonnie. "I mean, he had this trial and his divorce all within a two- to three-year period. The man was left with nothing. We were together, but he was totally devastated. And that trial went on for six days at a time when he could not afford to lose any income. I was supporting us for about the first five years until he got back on his feet. I had just started working at Nebraska AAA on commission, so I did not have a lot of money. It was pretty tough times."

Another distressing thing that happened to Manhart during this period was being victimized by a crime that not only stole something of his but violated a basic code of professional conduct, not to mention his trust. He believes a plant apparently acting on behalf of some of his dental opponents stole his calcium therapy patent right from under his nose. He suspects it was the work of a hygienist who worked briefly for him at the time. This alleged spy and thief was apparently directed to infiltrate his office in order to secret away the patent so it could be examined and copied.

"She stole that patent from a filing cabinet in my office, kept it for a couple weeks and then by an anonymous courier returned it to my office," he said with outrage. "I had had that patent in my files, stapled together, unfolded. It was a new copy. When I got it back, it was dog-eared, folded back on every page, the staples removed."

He cannot prove what happened or who was behind it all, but he has a pretty good idea. He said the incident was one in a series of suspicious episodes that put him on guard. For example, he once caught a dentist standing in his private office reading papers on his desk. Manhart walked in, saw what the snoop was up to, and intervened to stop him with a sharp reprimand on the impropriety of it all. Manhart said, "Another dentist told me a few years later that he had been asked by some dentists to go to work with me in order to get the patent, but that he would not do it, that he was insulted by the proposal and he turned them down flatly."

Manhart said the dirty tricks campaign directed at him was a disappointment but not a surprise. He knows the lengths some people are prepared to go in order to get an advantage or to silence a critic. He accepts it as a price of doing business.

"I mean, it was one of these struggles that you do not like but you have to live with," he said. Despite being the target of such foul play, he and Bonnie survived those tough times. What does not kill you, makes you stronger. Manhart never got his sweet revenge on the specialists who openly went after him in court, but he did gain a measure of vindication and at the same time send a message to his detractors.

"The biggest thing with the court case was we won it, we won the appeal, and no one has dared get near me again. You can be ostracized, which I was, and that was fine, I could take that, that is happened to me in other things. What's the big deal? But the full effect of it is a lot of dentists have been manhandled and really destroyed by specialists like this.

"Family dentists in California and in a lot of areas can hardly do anything because specialists go to court to testify against them if they try to do endodontics or periodontics or orthodontics. It has really gotten to be something fierce. As a result of my court case nobody has tried that with me, and I have made it very clear that I would go anywhere in this country to testify against one of those specialists. So, you see, I can play that game, too." To his credit, he has not yet.

Special interests failed to curtail Manhart and his treatments but they have succeeded in stymieing his research. Years ago he managed to do some research "quietly" at the University of Nebraska at Omaha biology department. He said he only got any research done then because he went around or avoided the dental establishment and its predisposed bias against calcium therapies.

"This was after years of dealing with organized dentistry and trying to get articles published and get research published on this. When you send your research papers to every dental journal in the world and no one wants to publish you, it gives you an idea they are not interested. In the interim somebody at my university published an article discrediting the use of calcium for root canal therapy. The article attempted to debunk what we were doing," he said. "The citations were longer than the article. I read this article closely, and it was not a case of the author having tried the calcium therapy and challenging it by saying it does not work and more research needs to be done, it was just a totally excessive review of literature that supported what the author was trying to say."

In other words, the article contained no controverting evidence. It was, in Manhart's opinion, just another shallow attempt to defame, to discredit, to discourage, to harass. Manhart actually invites anyone to challenge his findings, by saying, "If some dentist ever called and said, 'Manhart, this does not work, and I am going to learn it and do research and I am going to prove this does not work,' that would be the best thing to ever happen for everybody."

Instead of a scientific vetting of his work though, there has been only invective or silence and, worse yet, almost no opportunity for Manhart to formally present his findings to his American colleagues in print or presentation for the kind of real, honest, open dialogue and debate he wants.

"What I mind is that no one has come out with an article to try and show that what we are doing does not work," he said. "The best thing that could happen would be for someone else to do a study that replicates the same studies-therapies we have done because this is the way science works—teach me what you know, and teach me how to do it, and let me do it and confirm or challenge what you know. You look at physics, math, any science like that and that sort of thing is done. Or better yet, you have got an Einstein and a Kepler saying to each other, this is what I know, let me see what you know, and take it and go off on your own and keep going, even if you do not tell me what you are doing, keep going with it. Dentistry does not do that very easily, especially in this country.

"If this calcium treatment for gum disease does not work, well then what have I been doing? Have I been harming people all these years? Then why is it that people are not just pounding at this door demanding my license for all the damage I have done to them," he wonders.

The lack of general, widespread endorsement from his peers and the lack of an American Dental Association or American dental colleges' seal of approval for his work has made him cynical about his profession and embittered about the energy he expended trying to change a system he had no power or control or influence to affect. He says he is not cynical or bitter—rather, only telling it the way it is. But the words speak for themselves.

"If I were to talk to a group of dental students, one of the first things I would say is, 'If you ever discover anything, do not waste your time and energy ever trying to get your fellow dentists to approve it. Instead, work on your patients, go somewhere else and just enjoy life, enjoy your discoveries because you do not have a snowball's chance in hell of convincing other dentists that you are worth listening to.' My God, I was going all over the country wasting my time and energy trying to share this with these people, saying, 'Hey, take this home and use it, it is wonderful.' Now, I do not say that in a cynical way, there is nothing cynical about that, it is just common sense," Manhart said.

The more he talks about it, the more clean he comes with his true feelings and how it has been a process for him to go from militantly agitating his points of view in the face of stiff resistance to simply forging ahead with his work.

"Stop beating a dead horse is the conclusion I have come to," he said. "People take that to mean as if I am ready to throw up my hands and stop doing this. That is not true. What is true is, I have come to the realization I must stop beating my head against a dead horse trying to get that horse to understand what I am doing. Now I am focused on just continuing to work harder on what I am doing and sharing it with the people who benefit from it, namely, patients. I mean, I have gone through stages of being cynical and being pissed off and being upset with these guys, but I think I am through most of that."

RESEARCH

Rather than back off or quit in the face of skeptics and opponents, Manhart has kept right on plugging away. A couple different times he actually did arrange with the help of University of Nebraska at Omaha biology and chemistry faculty to do experiments in on-campus labs at Morrill Hall. He earned a bachelor's degree in biology from UNO around the same time, which was an expression of his wanting a deeper understanding of and grounding in the science behind the biological processes at work in calcium's interaction with the human body. The first study he did there was in the '80s.

"We put it together and we did it," he remembers. "Dr. Bill de Graw [former UNO biology chair] and Dan Sullivan [emeritus professor of chemistry] were wonderful about it. I remember Sullivan saying, 'Manhart, if you do this it sounds like this might harm someone.' I told him, 'Yeah, I know it sounds that way but I have been doing this for fifteen years and never harmed anybody, so it has to have some value, so let's do it quietly, and we did do it—on calcium. We did some human trials, taking blood from the finger before, during, and after the treatment with the calcium and the results were absolutely stunning.

"We theorized that it would raise the calcium level of the blood serum markedly for a short period of time, and it would gradually come down safely. What we were not ready for was that the calcium level of the serum stayed significantly higher, longer, and then came down. There was a significant increase over seven days period and that finding was absolutely stunning, because that tells us so much and it implies so much about, for example, potential osteoporosis treatments," he said.

"I knew we had something that we were so far ahead of the rest of dentistry in the world. It could have developed into wonderful research and a great name for the dental school, and that is why I told Bill Degraw, 'I want your name on this.' This is basic science and it should have led to clinical research at the dental school, which I would have been very proud to be part of."

That was in the early '80s and yet nothing more has ever come of it outside Manhart's own Calcium Therapy Institute. No follow-up, no publication, no nothing involving the university. Not for lack of trying.

"It was a wonderful little experiment that told us so dang much I could not wait to do the next step," he said. The next step after testing calcium levels in blood was a planned experiment with saliva. The protocol was to take saliva from a patient who had been treated with calcium— before, during, and after treatment. The study was about to commence when third parties interfered and put a stop to it. Manhart was taken aback because the study was just about to get under way when word came down that the protocol had to go before a review board and gain its approval before going forward.

"We went through the process of setting up the protocol and everything and there was no problem, and I did not have to jump through any hoops for anybody and neither did the UNO biology people," he said. "These are smart guys and they knew what I was doing. Well, all at once we had to go to the University of Nebraska's Human Subjects Committee because someone at the dental school said this is too dangerous. If you are going to do research on human subjects, the committee has to approve. And so we went through the process and I presented what I was doing to the committee and I was very impressed with their interest in what we were doing. Well, it came back we cannot do it, it is too dangerous.

"I countered with, 'Well, we did this similar thing with blood and all we want to do is take a swab of saliva. How can that be dangerous? And how can it be dangerous if I have done this for fifteen years and never hurt anyone?'"

The episode and Manhart's take on it also illustrates his appreciation for and frustration with the processes and systems of basic research. He wanted research carried out on calcium materials and applications of them at the same time he was treating patients with materials and applications that dental science had routinely done for nearly a century. He bristled at the notion of deferring treatment while the scientific method exhausted its protocols only in the United States.

He said, "If we had been very good little boys, we would still be doing the basic science of this whole thing and not treating patients. Or we probably would just be beginning in the last five years to treat patients because that whole process of doing the basic science—the lab work, the animal studies, the human studies—takes years."

The committee held firm in denying the study. Manhart did not take the decision lying down. "I said, 'I would like to challenge your decision and I would like to know who said

we cannot do it,' and we found out it was somebody at the dental school who is not even a dentist but a microbiologist or something like that. I said, 'I would like to challenge this and have it sent to other universities and have their boards see whether it is dangerous or not.' They sent it to Iowa, right to the guy who does not want calcium used this way, and he said it is too dangerous."

Manhart ascribes what happened to politics as usual in his field. "The American rationale they used does not make sense, but that was the rationale. They interpreted it the way they wanted to." On the off chance the committee reviewers may have been turned off by the idea of calcium hydroxide being used, Manhart took great pains to avoid that term in his protocol. In the final analysis, he said, "They just did not want it done."

"The only way I got another research project done [comparing mouth rinses] was to do it quietly in the UNO biology department where we did not need human subjects. We did that on bacteria and the results of that again were stunning. We measured the bacteria kill, how much bacteria are killed in a Petri dish over time. Basic science. It was wonderful to see what was going on. It led to understanding the products we were using, understanding what we were doing in the mouth. It told us a lot. Then we wanted to compare it to Listerine. We did that study. It was amazing. It told us a heckuva lot. The study was carried out under the direction of a microbiologist with his student lab assistants."

Manhart explained the rationale behind the mouthwash study: "If you have anything that is putting more toxins into the mouth and stimulating the activity of the bacterial level of the mouth, logically you are in trouble. There is something going on if you have a compound that controls that. Then logically it will follow that it will reduce the level of activity of bacteria, reduce the toxic level of the mouth, and as a result reduce decay and make a healthier mouth and gums. But that is dwelling on the microbial aspect of this. It should act slowly over a long period of time without harming the healthy tissues.

"There is a lot of difference between killing bacteria and controlling their growth. A lot of mainstream dental products kill bacteria and it is that mentality that we must kill bacteria as opposed to the bacteria are going to be there regardless, so let's simply control them and control them over time, not in milliseconds, like Listerine does. You kill things in milliseconds, you are not just killing bacteria. Something that will kill bacteria by the billions in a millisecond is something that will kill a lot more than bacteria.

"There are a lot of products like that out there. And the whole mentality of cleaning the teeth is to clean the food and the bacteria off and make it healthy that way. If you have a knife and you drive it into the skin, the chances are good that it is not just going to get that bullet out that is in there, but it is going to kill a lot of things around where that bullet is lodged and it is going to do it fast, and that is kind of what a quick-kill product is."

Manhart felt he had demonstrated enough results to formalize the research relationship with the university. Indeed, he did reach an agreement for continuing research there and yet no further work commenced. He attributes the standstill to more politics.

"Nothing has happened," he said. "It is the world of education. I spent a lot on legal fees to finalize a contract to do research again with the UNO biology department." The contract stipulates that he will provide ideas for the school to investigate and he will share access to the results. "That is the contract. The head of the department is very, very interested in doing it, and nothing has been done. I have politely called and asked when will you be ready, and when can we begin doing this. No reply. It just sits on the shelf," he said.

"When the periodontal guru at Penn State University published in the national dental journal that organized dentistry will 'put Keyes and Manhart on the shelf,' it was a life-career-making compliment to be mentioned in the same sentence with Dr. Paul Keyes, the pioneer in nonsurgical oral health. But I had no idea UNO had succumbed to Penn State in dental science. That is when I wrote the research committee that if this would have been about Nebraska football, the university would have picked it up instantly. The irony is that we have designed and we sell a product of calcium that could be used to help prevent athletic injuries. It is quite remarkable, but the UNL athletic department will not even respond to my offer of it. I think I will go to Penn State," he said.

The deadends that Manhart has continually encountered in the organized dentistry world, particularly what happened with the University of Nebraska, only reinforce his belief that he is considered persona non grata.

"That again proves to me that something happened that just put this on the shelf. It was just dropped. Those kinds of things are never put on paper and never made a record of, but you can judge it by the results and the results are zero. You see, what I learned and know as a fact is that no contact, no activity, no challenging of these ideas is the way to stop it," he said. "Maybe I am misreading dentistry as it is today, but I don't think so. It was certainly that way fifteen years ago and I don't think it has changed."

His intuition tells him that a higher-up determined he is "not the right person" to do the research. In other words, he is not a specialist. "If I were the right person—like a periodontist in Lincoln or the dentist in Colorado, you are damn right that it would get done. What I am willing to do is do the research with the periodontists in my school, the University of Nebraska, on their patients, teaching them everything I know. It is just that I want my name on something."

He suspects the university would prefer to cut him out of the equation altogether and let their own faculty and dental school reap the rewards of the research without having to share anything with Manhart and his Institute. "It is as simple as that," he said. "These are the stupidest things scientists will fight over—who gets their name on top. Either publish or perish. It does not matter who is on top. The person who is on top is the patient, and that is what they cannot figure out."

For Manhart it represents yet another frustrating encounter with the organized dentistry world. "I spent all kinds of money making a contract. It was exceptionally expensive to have that done properly by my attorney and their attorneys and the head of the university's Human Research Committee."

He believes he is being railroaded, so to speak, because, as the dental colleges see it, he has "no credentials" from their narrow point of view. In his own version of point-counterpoint Manhart simulated the questions his detractors raise and his answers, point by point:

"Now get this, I have credentials to teach what I practice and what I have been practicing for forty-plus years. Sure you have a lot of dentists who practice that long, but I have been teaching and practicing endodontics and periodontics to an enormous degree, more than probably any dentist in this city, other than specialists, that I know of. Well, yeah, but he just does that because he enjoys it, they will say. It is true I enjoy it but I have also been published and what's more I have been published in the top dental journal in the world (The Triple O). Oh, well, that was a quirk, they will say, and that work was not really well documented. Okay, then, give me one other dentist in the world who has spent all these years doing root canal therapy and periodontal therapy, full-scale, with calcium materials. You might find one.

"Give me one dentist who has been doing this for as long as I have. You ain't going to find anybody. Dr Steg and I are now the two top experts in calcium treatment in dentistry of any kind in the world, and over the years we have found that calcium materials can be used in every single dental specialty."

Steg agrees with Manhart that many specialists are loathe to accept new ideas and new therapies in the field "coming from somebody else," as in general dentists like himself and Manhart. Periodontists tend to embrace new ideas only from fellow periodontists, he confirmed. Steg believes that if the calcium therapies discovered by him and Manhart were advanced by specialists rather than general practitioners like themselves, things would be very different. "If this were developed and such by a periodontist, there would be widespread acceptance right now," Steg said.

When Manhart and Steg have presented their calcium program before colleagues at dental conventions and conferences, Steg said there has been "more interest in it than against it by a wide margin." The few opponents generally are specialists. Steg said the reception by dentists and hygienists at endodontic and periodontic clinics conducted by Manhart has also been consistently positive.

Steg said, "We used to conduct these trainings right in the office here where [Manhart] would be treating patients with calcium materials for root canals. We would have an all-day seminar and dentists would come in and participate and view the actual procedure. There would be lecture notes all about the technique, and they would get a continuing education credit for that."

"When I started presenting clinics or lectures around the country," said Manhart, "it was really exciting to hear how many general dentists were interested in it. I could go to any state or regional convention and be pretty much an attraction out of the others who were presenting. It was when some other things came up that the specialists got into serious opposition to this, and it is still present today, but they have to be more careful about it, being opposed to it, because they went so far as to take me to court and they lost and they made fools of themselves. You know, it was like after that they just left me alone, and so the opposition is more subtle now," he said.

"It is couched in a lot of stuff like 'change is hard' and all that kind of phony stuff. You know, if you do not want to do something, you can think of ten reasons why you should not. Or if you take it as an affront to your position or your income, you can think up ten reasons immediately why it is bad," Manhart said.

Steg confirmed that Manhart is effective in clinic settings where he gets to be the expert or promoter. Manhart now does some of that clinical training online. Participating dentists complete seven online sessions with him to become recognized by the Calcium Therapy Institute as being trained in its therapies.

There is no doubt Manhart is in his element when talking, lecturing, proclaiming, demonstrating. He has refined his conversational communication style from years of theatre, Rotary, teaching, and practicing. He knows what it means to be on and in-the-moment. He understands how to project his voice so that everyone in the room can hear him, and then for effect, he knows how to speak just above a whisper or else raise his voice just below a shout and yet still make himself understandable.

You may not like what he is saying, but he will get your attention. This consummate communicator can easily work from notes or just as easily wing it with an extemporaneous riff. Always a quick thinker on his feet, he is not easily thrown by a question or an interruption, or, on those occasions when he is addressing dentists and a specialist gets up to challenge him, he knows how to handle a heckler.

Manhart fondly recalls those halcyon days when he and Dr. Steg conducted clinics for dentists right out of their office. Those kinds of moments are among the times when he feels most alive and useful as a working professional. The partners did them together, but make no mistake about it, Manhart was the center of attention. He did the procedures on the patients and Steg assisted.

"When Tom and I were teaching root canals or endodontics in the office," Manhart said, "we would bring in maybe eight dentists at a time. We would do a root canal—a molar root canal—as a hands-on training and so many of them said, 'How can you do that with us here? How can you do such a complicated, delicate thing on your patient with us all standing around gawking at you?' They could not do it—I am serious. Tom cannot do it. Tom is capable of doing it, he's capable of doing better work than I can do. But he probably would not want to be watched."

Too much pressure for most practitioners. Manhart on the other hand excels under the lights, whether the examination lamp or the stage lights, and he thrives before a live audience watching his every move. Flop sweat be damned. What does not kill you, makes you stronger.

"Man, when you got other people really watching, that is not easy to do, and it really bothered me but my gosh you do that and they just go nuts, they just love it and our patients say this. 'We're through? We're done? My God, you did a root canal on me in twenty minutes? You can't—nobody has done that.' And, you know, it is not that Tom is fast or I am real fast. It is that we took the eight hundred things we were taught in dental school for doing a root canal, and we refined it down to maybe a couple hundred."

These clinics demonstrated in a real-time, intimate way the distilled calcium root canal treatment Manhart and Steg had arrived at after decades of practice.

He explains, "You numb the tooth and you drill a hole in the top, You get into the tooth as much as you can. You go down into the root canals and you file and clean them. You are putting medication in there or a cleansing agent. You clean it and dry it and you use points with calcium on it and you insert the points. You have this inert latex point that is carrying calcium and kind of distributing it along that canal and that calcium is so friendly to the tooth it does several things. It is antibacterial, it is anti-inflammatory, it is analgesic, it is alkaline and loaded with calcium and zinc. It does a lot of good things. That is what we use and one of the best things is that it stimulates healing of the whole area.

"You do the work, you seal it, and you get the heck out. And the neat thing is it is reversible, it can be taken out. In other words, the first time you put it in gently so that two weeks later you can take it out easily, and then you go in and you file again and you clean again and this time you seal it tightly and you leave very little of the calcium but just enough to treat it again. Then you double seal that latex with a filling of some kind. What you are doing over this period of time is getting the end of the tooth to heal itself. It is like you mechanically close it, and over a few months the root tip closes and forms a scab that is healthy, so you have got something that is closed at both ends. It is rendered neutral and the bone decides to keep it.

"The treatment of choice [among most dentists] is to use a cement material that when you put your point in it hardens so hard that you will never get that point out. Ours, on the other hand, is reversible—you can back off and do it again even years later if needed."

As with most of the calcium therapies Manhart and Steg use, the root canal procedure is minimally invasive. So much so, he said, "that almost half of the time we go into the tooth without even any anesthesia, especially on the second appointment. The second appointment I go in, take out all that I put in, file a little better, clean a little better, make it a little more accurate, and then seal it up real tight and then double seal the top of the tooth. That is it, you are through. In other words, we do it in two appointments."

That approach flies in the face of mainstream root canal work that does almost everything in one sitting. Manhart believes taking extra time has its benefits "because almost anytime you are dealing with a root canal, it has been dying for a long time and so it is going to take more than one hit, one treatment, and that is going to take time. It takes time for things to get better, for healing to occur, and so we do that second appointment two weeks later usually to allow things to have calmed down and everything. The patient is even chewing on the tooth by then. We go in and repeat it, seal it up real good, and that is the final treatment. And we do all that at the cost of doing one root canal."

The majority of Steg's tenure at the Calcium Therapy Institute has been a period of discovery and productivity. Both he and Manhart enjoy busy, fruitful practices. Their ongoing thirty-year partnership is almost unheard of these days.

"The staff has been with us forever it seems, Sherry, Mary Kay, and Julie, who came to the office a quarter century ago," Manhart mused.

Steg has also witnessed the battles and struggles that Manhart has waged and the wear and tear these conflicts have caused them. He can recall a couple instances when he saw the normally gregarious Manhart at his lowest.

The first depression Steg observed had to do "with that lawsuit and the testimony of these different periodontists on the patient he had treated. They tried to make a case out of nothing. The patient never lost a tooth, had not had any damage to herself in any way. She just did not pay her bills and we turned her over to collection. Then she went to somebody else, to specialists, and they were just looking for something to get a lawsuit against him to stop him. They had all these experts, professors from the University of Nebraska Dental College, to testify. They tried to say, 'Oh, this person needs tens of thousand of dollars' worth of work to get her mouth into shape.' And Manhart won. The jury did not see the plaintiff's claims.

"It was just a fabricated lawsuit by a lawyer that was trying to make some money but did not know what he was doing, and a university that was trying to get Manhart, and the truth came out."

The other low point involved the second research study Manhart was doing at UNO that university officials put a stop to. "I think they were scared we were going to cause harm to patients. That was a big disappointment to him," Steg said.

Preceding these setbacks was what happened at Creighton University, when Manhart was let go after officials there accused him of essentially preaching heresy by espousing therapies and techniques unapproved by organized American dentistry. Steg supports Manhart's account of what transpired, which amounted to a betrayal.

"He had done studies and research on the use of different calcium materials in foreign countries," Steg said. "After seeing the results of calcium materials in his own work, he was trying to incorporate that into the curriculum of the endondontic department at Creighton, and he met strong resistance there, and it actually resulted in them terminating him," said Steg. "That was a big, big disappointment. That I think kind of solidified his mindset against specialists and how they do things."

Steg said that while Manhart can come across as a zealot, which may turn some off or rub some the wrong way, there really is not anything about the personality of the man or the way he advocates for calcium that makes him a target. No, Steg believes Manhart's dilemma is that he is the proverbial fly in the ointment and the persistent irritant who is thus deemed a troublemaker and so must be silenced or squashed by the-powers-that-be. "They would be going after anyone that was advancing what he is advancing, but he is not intimidated by that, and so I suppose that is even more irritative to them," according to Steg.

That and the fact Manhart just will not go away or disappear into the good night, at least not quietly or without a good fight. "What is most amazing about Dr. Manhart is that I would have given up long ago fighting these guys," said Steg. "I would have thrown my hands up and said, 'The hell with it,' but he doesn't. He keeps on. It is like you are at a carnival in one of these bumper cars and all of a sudden you bump into another car, and bounce off ... Well, he will go in a slightly different direction full steam ahead and he will keep probing and probing and he keeps advancing. What I most admire about him is his stick-to-it-iveness. I mean, when he meets resistance, he keeps going. When other people would quit, he keeps going. That is a trait that is necessary for success."

Steg can only speculate what makes Manhart so determined to persevere. "Well, I don't know, maybe it has something to do with his father. His father had an inventive mind and he invented a rotary lawnmower. He had it developed, he was making some, selling some, but he did not have a patent on it and some other company got a patent on it and it took off, and I think that may have some influence about Dr. Manhart carrying on."

10

Bonnie, Marathon Tennis, the GOP, and a Life Together

Just as Tom Steg is the right counterbalance to Manhart in his professional life, wife Bonnie Gill is the perfect foil in Manhart's personal life. She is a smart, tough, beautiful "broad" with a career and life all her own, and she has no problem cutting him down to size when his inflated ego needs it. But she knows his ego is an extension of the unbridled passion he has for his work. Like Steg, she marvels at his persistence and now better understands what fuels it.

She said, "I could never stay as dedicated to a cause as he is through all the drama, but he has a real need to be famous, a real need to be great. He has the big ego. Me, I give everything up too easily. If it is too much work, I am out of here. It is not my drive, it is not my passion, but it is his and I am glad it is. I often tell him, you are so lucky to have worked in a profession for decades and still be in love with it. He is in love with it. I mean, his goal is to die working on somebody. My daughter is a dentist and she does not feel that way at all. She is looking for the day when she can get out. I mean, she likes her work okay and everything, but ten years into it she was ready to get out."

When Manhart complains about how tough he has had it, Bonnie reminds him that she has not had the privileged life he has enjoyed. "I am a South Omaha scrapper with the wrong name and the wrong family who had to fight for everything I got," she said, "whereas he was tall, dark, and handsome and came from a prominent family and became a dentist. Just a totally different life."

As wives often do with high-octane husbands who get a bit carried away with themselves, she feels it is her job to put him in his place or to force him to look at things from a different perspective. It is an inevitable but thankless role in a relationship. It can leave the wife feeling she is a nag or a wet blanket. The husband can be made to feel he is a boy not a man. A wife should not be a mother to her mate.

"I always feel like I am his devil's advocate. I am his worst critic, I am his hardest critic and his biggest naysayer and I hate that," said Bonnie. "I have really refrained a lot from that in the last years."

They are very different people in most ways, according to Bonnie, which is why she and others who know them sometimes wonder "how two totally opposites got together." She is the practical one. He is the dreamer. She is organized. He is somewhat the absent-minded professor. She looks after certain responsibilities that, if he were left to his own devices, would not get done. Compensating for their differences, she said, is the fact that "we both love the arts, so that is in our favor, and we both have high, high energy levels."

She said with the kids and when they go on vacation, she is all about relaxing and having fun, part of which is letting her hair down, having a few cocktails, and partying with other people, often family; whereas, he is perfectly content being off by himself alone curled up with a good book. It is not so much Manhart is incapable of being spontaneous, it is just that his impulsive streak is wired less socially and more scientifically.

Some of Bonnie and Mark's eighteen grandchildren.

"We go [on vacation] and does he sit with us, does he yuck it up and have beers and margaritas? No, he is at the other end of the pool reading quietly, deciding what his next project is going to be. 'Relax already,' I tell him. But he relaxes in front of the TV. He is just different. I am younger than he is, and so I kind of miss that craziness every once in a while, not that I have to have a steady diet of it, but I want it once and a while. When we first got married he said, 'Oh, I wish we would have hooked up twenty years ago.' And I said, 'In all fairness to your ex-wife, it would never have lasted, I could never have raised kids with you.' I would have been a nut case if I would have had six or eight kids, and he decided he was going to just pick up and go to Venezuela and work on the natives, which he did once. He just picked up and went. I would have killed him," she said.

There is that part of her that wishes he would be more sociable. "In my first marriage we had a couple we did everything with, and I could never see Mark and I doing that." Then again, they have the theatre and their huge appetite for life. Alas, one cannot live on the arts and adrenalin alone. While he is chronically wrapped up in his practice, in new areas of calcium exploration, and in his plays, she is disciplined enough to do a theatre project here or a music gig there but to stay consistently focused on attending to the business of ensuring their futures.

She has maintained her jobs as an advertising salesperson and sometime travel writer because the work provides health insurance coverage for both of them. She is the one who socks money away in a retirement fund so they will have a nest egg to live on in their Golden Years. Without her foresight they would be in a far less comfortable and secure financial situation than they are today.

"I am working so that we both have benefits and I have saved all the retirement. He is not interested, he lives for today," Bonnie said. "He is the idea person, and I have often felt like the elephant's helper. Not so much anymore because in any relationship you split apart and I get my areas and he gets his areas, but when we first started with tennis and the theatre (the Grande Olde Players) I was always into those."

MARATHON TENNIS

Mark and Bonnie have always been active, and for a time the two regularly played tennis together as a way to stay fit and to socialize. They both love the game. Neither was an accomplished player, however. He was a bit more advanced, so they found all the miss-hit balls and breaks in action a real impediment to getting any good, sustained exercise. After every couple of swings it seemed, they were stopping to retrieve the ball or to set up for the next serve. Looking for a way to keep their heart rates up, the two devised their own version of the game called Marathon Tennis. It was all in fun, but they took it seriously enough to give it some real thought and to draw up an entire set of rules.

"That was one of those crazy things Bonnie and I did that was really kind of neat," Manhart said. "This was back when we were still kind of getting to know each other. We made up this silly thing where we would play till 21, and if the ball was hit out, you could still hit it, but you took a point. We would go on and on, stroke after stroke, and sometimes you were so tired you would just let the damn ball go in order to take a break. We really got our aerobic, cardiovascular work in doing that. God, we would play a game of that and we would get more exercise than if we had played an entire set of regular tennis. We would be sweating like crazy. It got us warmed up right away."

He said onlookers stared at them as if they were crazy, which only added to the kick the couple got from doing it. One of the reasons they came up with this personalized form of tennis was that for their tastes the traditional game was too rigid and staid. Leave it to Mark and Bonnie to loosen things up.

THE THEATRE

The Grande Olde Players played a big role in the pair cementing a friendship that evolved into something more after they were divorced from their first spouses. "The theatre really did bring us together," Bonnie said, "because it was a true passion." Much like Manhart adored theatre but was a neophyte at doing it, when he joined the ranks of the Norton Theatre, Bonnie was a fan but novice when she began working with Manhart on theatre projects.

"I did a little in high school but I was never a big theatre geek. But I always loved it and music I always loved, too," she said.

The theatre did not come between them and their spouses.

"We had very happy marriages in the beginning but something died along the way," she said. "We were both trying to get our spouses involved in the theatre and it was obvious they did not want any part of it. A lot of people in both of our families felt that the Grande Olde Players broke up our marriages, and they hated the theatre and never supported it. Don't you find it interesting that most of our family members have never seen us perform on stage? I think that is very interesting. What is that all about? But Mark and I both know that the Grande Olde Players is maybe one of six reasons that broke up the marriages."

Bonnie likes that she, Mark, and his ex-wife Mary "are all friends now. Not bosom buddies, but friends. It has been great."

After her first marriage Bonnie was hardly eager to jump into another and risk opening old wounds that had not even healed yet. "I was really scared because I was single longer than he was single. I was scared to get out, and when I got out I was scared to get back in. I kept saying, 'Can't we just live together?' But it worked out. I was married eighteen years the first time, and we have been married twenty-three, so I am the marrying kind I guess. But this one has been way easier because we can agree to disagree. That is one thing I know about Mark and I and it is so refreshing."

On the other hand, she said his quixotic nature can be exasperating for someone literal as herself. She said his outside-the-box thinking sometimes makes him his own worst enemy.

"This is what I cannot figure out about Mark—he is intelligent and he does know what he is doing. But he always says two plus two equals five and I am not there with him, because I am like, two plus two equals four. I need a linear world. It better be logical for me," she said. "When I watched him run for City Council I would go to these coffees or whatever they were, and I would almost crawl in a shell from embarrassment because I would think, you are not addressing what they are asking—you are not answering the questions. And it would just drive me crazy." She said she would tell him, "I am not following you on this. What are you talking about? You are going on too long."

She said when people would come up to her after one of his addresses and comment, " 'Oh, he has such a different wit, I just love it,' she would reply, 'Well, I'm glad you do because I do not understand it one bit.' But yeah, that's me, I have to be very literal, I have to be very exact."

Mark will not be boxed in by the norm. Sometimes his overbearing manner causes tensions outside their relationship. It did at the Grande Olde Players.

"We had some problems with him in the theatre," she said, "where he would always come in very nice but then be erratic. Mark is not a big person on consensus, which I did not understand. On the flip side of that, I could always understand where he was coming from. He was paying the bills, there were people that were undermining other people.

"One thing he did do in the theatre, and this is another thing I admire about him, was always be very open to letting people get involved. But he would be open to his own detriment, in a way like a little kid. If he would like you, he could just go overboard and give you all kinds of responsibilities and bring you into his inner circle without testing you along the way. And then he would have this problem because you and he would not see eye-to-eye on everything, yet you were in there and he did not know how to get you out," she explained.

Long-time Grande volunteer Lew Ryan confirmed that Manhart could be difficult to deal with if not approached the right way. Among Ryan's many duties was videotaping the shows. He recalled once that an actress-attorney had, without telling him or Manhart, enlisted a young man to do the videography for a show. It was fine with Lew, but when Manhart found out the arrangement was to make copies for her family and friends, he turned defensive and protective about it and in no uncertain terms refused the young man's services and the volunteer's meddling because he knew what Ryan did not—that copyright laws prohibit such recordings. This conflict later led to a lawsuit against the theatre by the attorney's bedfellow over voluntary work at the theatre for which the couple wanted payment. The theatre spent thousands of dollars in legal fees and finally got the case dropped.

"It was nonsense," said Manhart. "None of us got paid for our huge investments of time at the theatre."

Ryan said, "Another thing too I saw many times: To get Mark to do something you want done, you walk up and discuss it with him, you do not walk up and say, 'I want this done and I want it done now,' because just brace yourself for a ton of concrete blocks to drop on you. He is really tough, he is really dedicated. He's the same age I am and he was there at the theatre punching, working every day, just like it was his full-time job. He has got a lot of get up and go and he gets things done it seems like. Now I do not always agree with the way he does some things, but ..."

There was at least one topic Ryan learned to avoid discussing around Manhart. "He is a staunch Democrat, I am a Republican, and I learned right off the bat I do not even want to discuss politics with him. I just keep my mouth shut, go in the other room, and hide." Any talk about religion with Manhart around sent Ryan scurrying for cover, too.

Manhart appreciates the irony of his beloved theatre's acronym having been GOP, when he was and is anything but conservative.

Bonnie sometimes wonders how she and Manhart have managed to make their relationship work. One way is to maintain clearly drawn boundaries and roles. For example, when they did the Grande together, she carved out a niche for herself as a producer, director, marketer, and business manager, only rarely venturing on stage to perform, which was more his domain. Her favorite on-stage role was as Maggie in *The Man Who Came to Dinner*. Her favorite directing experience was helming the theatre's acclaimed production of Neil Simon's *Lost in Yonkers*.

She also indulged her love of music through the musicals she worked on and by launching the Jazz on Stage program at the theatre, which featured local jazz professionals in concert on Sunday evenings following an open jam session in the lobby. She often joined in, playing the keyboards alongside some of the area's best cats, from Joey Gulizia to Robert Glaser, and silky smooth vocalists such as Suzy Thorne.

As usual, Manhart preferred doing a little bit of everything, from acting to directing to running the place. He was just as comfortable out front as he was behind the curtain. "Mark is wonderful on stage. I always say he is really a scientist and an actor at his downright core, where I am the director," Bonnie said. "I like to be behind the scenes, I do not like that limelight. I had bit parts because I was too shy. I am still not too comfortable on stage."

Bonnie playing at one of their home jazz soirees.
Leo Komar, Bonnie, and renowned artist Jerry Jacoby

Not everyone would agree about Manhart's acting ability. After all, just because you say you are an actor or cast yourself in a play does not mean you are any good at it. Or, as Grande veteran actor/director James Thorson put it, "This didn't mean that Mark could act for sour apples. He forgot lines on par with Jerry Vegner, who was legendary for forgetting lines, once even an entire page of dialogue."

When a production of *Love, Sex and the IRS* that Manhart was directing went over big, it was extended, but one of the actors could not stay with the show. Thorson picked up the rest of the story: "So Mark cast himself in the part of the priest as I recall. He almost had an uprising on his hands, as we [the cast] had a sense of ownership by this time, and we did not want Mark blundering and spoiling 'our play.' Fortunately, he got his lines all right and everything went well for the final week, but we were sweating it for a while."

Thorson said the Grande Olde Players troupe was a family that had its riffs and tiffs, but the members always seemed to come together when it counted. He can recall many nights when things did not go according to script, from players missing their stage entrance cues and actors on stage being left to hang out to dry, frantically trying to fill time, to most infamously the lead actress in a play (another attorney in real life) who got arrested just before opening night.

"She was trying a case, got smart with the judge and he tossed her in jail," said Manhart. In classic show-must-go-on tradition the mother of a boy cast in the play went on in the missing lead's place, with absolutely no rehearsal time, and somehow it all worked out.

"The reviewer gave us high marks for doing what community theatre does best: improvise in the face of panic," said Thorson.

Mark and Bonnie have written and directed works together and those collaborations bring into relief their different approaches to things. "Whenever we go do a thing together, he loves to work off the cuff and I am like a nervous wreck because I have to have everything rehearsed," she said.

More than a few Grande veterans say that where Bonnie is a stickler for actors getting their lines down verbatim, Mark plays it loose with dialogue. Thorson said a free rein is fine but too much liberty can be a bad thing.

Bonnie acknowledges that the couple's work in theatre is more a self-taught labor of love than it is a career, which accounts for the fact that among Omaha's professional theatre community the couple has a spotty reputation. "The main thing we have against us is that neither one of us has a theatre degree. We are not educated in it. It is a hobby," she said. No one, however, questions their dedication. They put themselves and their own time, money, labor, and reputation on the line, after all, with the Grande Olde Players.

She said she always had the impression the Grande was widely regarded as "a loner" amateur theatre company off doing its own thing. "Most of the theatre people in town do not really know a lot about us."

Part of that fringe status, she said, was a result of Mark never wanting to join Omaha's Theatre Arts Guild, which for his taste smacks too much of the cronyism he found distasteful in the dental organizations he once belonged to. "He joined it once and he thought it was a bunch of bullshit," Bonnie said of his dalliance with TAG. She said just as Manhart could be too quick to judge an organization or a person, he sometimes had an inflated opinion of the Grande. "He always used to say we had the finest little theatre in Omaha, and I would say, 'Will you stop it, we do not, what we have is the finest little theatre facility in Omaha.'"

She said the theatre's on-stage product was a mixed bag. "Our production of *Lost in Yonkers* that I directed got a review from Jim Delmont of the *Omaha World-Herald* that said, 'Look out Omaha Community Playhouse because you have got your work cut out for you if you are going to be able to match this *Lost in Yonkers.*' That show just fell into place. I had an off-Broadway actress in the lead, I had a great script, everything worked out. But we had some real dogs, too."

From the perspective of Thorson, the Grande provided more than merely a theatre outlet but a batch of personal enrichment and cross-generational socialization opportunities for seniors.

Thorson said, "Small-time community theatre was a place to be creative, to grow, to be bad, and for people who were not actors to become actors. John Gondring, who was a disaster as a radio announcer in *The Sunshine Boys* was by a few years later the star of Agatha Christie's *An Unexpected Guest* and did a great job. During the dress rehearsal, John had to deliver a long soliloquy to the French doors, only to look up and see me behind them, looking back with my finger hanging out of my fly. He started to cry. He did the twenty actual performances with his eyes tightly shut while delivering those lines. There were a number of people who began with GOP who went on to big parts with the Omaha Community Playhouse. Some of our plays, such as *Noises Off* and *Love, Sex and the IRS,* were the best theatre in town during their runs."

Bonnie said that when she and Mark got involved in the Great Plains Theatre Conference, she assumed that the work they did at the Grande was not so well thought of by theatre professionals in the community. To her surprise, she said, "I found out differently." It turned out she and Mark and the Grande had their admirers among that serious thespian crowd. "The conference's manager, Rob Baker, had a lot of respect for us and even more after we did work with him."

Manhart's short plays *Pickwick's Dilemma* and *Cootie Blues* have been read in lab settings at the conference. He has also served as a short play panelist and as a director of several short plays at the conference. Bonnie has served as narrator for the pieces Manhart directed and she essayed parts in two of them, appearing as Jill/Sister Innocence in his own *Cootie Blues.*

Theatre also serves as a shared activity that helps the couple maintain a healthy balance in their lives. Just how important is theatre to them? "Huge," said Bonnie. "Theatre is like an opiate. I have had the experience myself of being so dog tired and then I go to rehearsal and it just vanishes. That is the effect it has if it is your thing and it is definitely my thing and Mark's thing. We like it."

If they let it, the Grande Olde Players could have caused a split because for a time the two were working in close confines and frequently butting heads over things. "Again, it was his identity, his baby, and it was our baby, too, because we started it together. But after five years of us coming together to the theatre in one car and then me walking home from the theatre because I would get mad at him," she said, she finally let him have the reins to himself so as to avoid those pitfalls that befall many couples that try working together.

Veteran theatre volunteer Lew Ryan said that Bonnie and Mark remained a volatile mix at the theatre but that they knew how to fight, get it out of their system, and then move as if nothing had happened. "They disagreed a lot and Bonnie did not hold back," he said. Venting is one of her relief mechanisms and Ryan noted that her spouse knew best to ride it out rather than try and fight it. "She just plain tells it like it is, and a lot of times I have seen Mark just sit there and take it. I think he knows better than to stick his hand in a wolf's mouth."

She recounted the time she laid into Mark after he had had a quadruple bypass and on doctor's orders was supposed to be lying in bed taking it easy, but when she went to the theatre she found instead, much to her chagrin, him moving a piano with someone else. She exploded.

"Every four-letter word came out of my mouth," she said. After calming down, the tirade was over and forgotten. Besides, she knew it was just another example of his "stubborn" streak coming into play. "We have managed to work through all this and we do not have nearly the blow-ups we had. It's funny, we would have all these blow-ups but I would still stick with him. They were all superficial things. The core of the person was somebody I could still respect and still like, even love." Another lesson the couple learned was not to bring their disputes or upsets home with them.

The Grande had a long and fruitful run, but ultimately it became impractical for the couple to keep it going. A new heating, ventilation, and air conditioning system was needed but the building's owner-landlord, Lund Co., was also asking for a five- to ten-year lease, during which time needed overhaul would be addressed. That would have meant going forward without the new HVAC system for a longer window of time than Mark and Bonnie desired, and it would have meant a longer commitment to keep the theatre than the couple was prepared to make.

Jason Ruegg, a brokerage associate for Lund, publicly stated the theatre had been a great tenant and an asset to the Plaza 90 strip mall it shared space in since 1991. "It's sad to see them go, and we wish them well," he told an *Omaha World-Herald* staff writer.

When all was said and done, then, the combination of ever-escalating costs to operate and upgrade the facility, not to mention the rising cost of mounting productions, combined with the new lease stipulation and a shrinking pool of volunteers and members made it clear the theatre's best days were behind it.

News of the closing made the local daily. Bonnie was quoted as saying, "We are choosing not to sign a new lease. We just had too many financial and staffing problems to keep going."

The theatre's guest jazz concerts and performing arts productions helped the bottom line, but in the end it was not enough. When the company notified longtime supporters of plans to vacate, the couple was inundated with calls. "When we put the figures together and decided to close, it was really hard on everyone," Mark said. "But we have accomplished more by an enormous amount than we dreamed we could. We want to go out with our heads up."

He put the closing in perspective. "Our matron/ reservationist for twenty years, Colene Moreno, said it all: 'You can be proud that you accomplished what you set out to do—make a place for the grand generation in Omaha theatre.'"

Remnants of the theatre remain in bits and pieces, from seats to curtains, salvaged by collectors. "So, in our final season we produced one of our best seasons in twenty years, closed it down, and gave away all anyone would take," said Manhart. "We are still finding places for what's left. The memories are another huge book, which we have started and want to do as a grateful couple who experienced a lot of great adventures we want to share as thanks. A group of the old-timers meets about monthly. The GOP still lives on as a company and family."

Thorson said the feat that Manhart pulled off in making the Grande a reality and in keeping it viable for as long as he did is to be commended. It is not often someone throws caution to the wind in order to indulge a passion that he or she can only enjoy by sharing with others. Theatre is, after all, a communal thing. One cannot make theatre alone. Even if one could, where is the fun in that anyway?

No, theatre is a living, breathing, moment-by-moment experience made by the people on stage, behind the curtain, and in the seats. It is all about the energy and ideas exchanged in the ephemeral interaction that goes on in a certain time and space, among a certain group of people, never to be repeated in quite that same way again. That is the magic of it all. It is a chemistry thing, not so unlike the chemical combinations Manhart makes in discovering new calcium materials or products. The unpredictable magic of live theatre is like the mercurial Manhart himself, liable to go in some direction you did not expect.

Just like his forming the Calcium Therapy Institute was a leap of faith and intuition, so was forming the Grande Olde Players, and the theatres that preceded it. So it was with every play he directed or produced. In each instance, Manhart had the courage of his convictions to not only put his money where his mouth was but to put his financial well-being and reputation at stake.

Thorson, the professor who got reeled in to being an actor, jotted down his reflections on the Grande, which sound a lot like a tribute:

"Early on, when making the big jump from the little Phoenix Club to a much bigger venue on 90th Street, Mark realized that he was taking on personal financial responsibility for a real commitment, one that involved considerable risk. I suspect that he underwrote the theater to the tune of thousands with no complaint, because even a good run hardly did more than pay the rent. When the new headquarters was being planned, he asked me and, I presume, a few others to sign on as financial guarantors should the thing flop. Thank God it did not, and we did a lot of things well over the years, gave a lot of old people a real kick, and made life interesting for the rest of us. Thanks to an energetic, creative, and altruistic man for doing something out of the ordinary."

When the old gang still get together, they reminisce about the high old times there. "About twenty of us still meet for birthday parties or any excuse we can generate," said Manhart. Grande veterans Keith Homan, Lew Ryan, and Dave Kistler convene their own breakfast club at a local restaurant, where their talk inevitably turns to the theatre, where they invested their time and talent and treasure.

Actor Keith Homan said he misses the Players. "Very much. I hated to see them fold up." But he is realistic enough to understand its time had come. "It had to."

Lew Ryan is sure that closing the theatre had to be tough on Manhart. "I didn't think he showed it on the surface but I think he must have felt it deep inside." As if it needed confirming, Manhart said, "I miss the theatre passionately. That is why I can think of the loss for only a few minutes. Then, I sit down and the thought passes, and the rest is for another publication. The most fulfilling thing about my involvement in theatre was to show that the world *is* a stage, and it is more rewarding to realize it in different ways than to be lost in a black hole of politics or religion."

Ryan is right though. Manhart can be hard to read because he can disguise and deflect his emotions so well and because he always has some new venture to occupy him.

"His mind is like a whole bunch of wheels up there," said Ryan, "and once he is done with one thing, he is on to the next project. When we made the decision we were going to close it, he was already thinking what his next project was. He cannot let grass grow under his feet at all. The minute we decided we were closing, he was out there with his resume."

"I was out looking for another venue for the Grande Olde Players," said Manhart.

Being a stage vagabond without a home theatre to go to was a reality Manhart had not had to confront all that time he had the Grande. Since it was his playhouse, he never had to worry about being without something to do in theatre. Without the Grande, he is a bit adrift these days but, as Ryan indicated, Manhart wasted no time in finding a new outlet for his passion by directing a show at the Chanticleer Theater in Council Bluffs. He later directed To Kill a Mockingbird there. Manhart has also experienced the other side of the coin by finding out that some theatres are not interested in his directing for them. Rejection comes with the territory. His thick skin can take it.

Meanwhile, Ryan and his coffee-klatch mates share their own take on what precipitated the theatre's closing. "Everybody got too old," said Homan. "The grand old players started dying off, and one thing and another" led to its demise. Ryan added, "Another thing, the membership was dying off and we were not replacing them." The aging theatre population is a concern for every stage venue these days in this era of online social networking and text messaging, when virtual reality is replacing actual nights out on the town for things like live theatre.

Manhart said the theatre is no more but "the Grande Olde Players Company and name are still ours. We are doing what we can occasionally, writing more." One way a facet of the theatre may live on is music concerts. The Grande organized and hosted a series of concerts under the banner Jazz on Stage, which ended when the theatre closed. Mark and Bonnie want to start the series up again as soon as they can find a patron and a place. "So who knows what lurks in the shadows?" he said.

He has also been consulting someone about a possible new theatre venue starting up in mid-town Omaha.

ON THE FRONTLINES WITH MANHART, IN HIS CORNER

Away from theatre, Bonnie has been there through thick and thin with her man. She has even lent a hand with various aspects of getting his dental work ready for publication and assisting him with the education programs he offers colleagues.

She said, "I used to be much involved. I did research on papers he was submitting for publication. I helped him edit stuff. Then I traveled with him for about a year or two when he was training some dentists around the country. I did the clinics with him in Iowa. He had a lot of people interested in Iowa years ago. I saw how good he was with his hands versus some people who are just all thumbs."

She also saw how perhaps he did not sell his therapies or follow up with clinic attendees as effectively as he could have, thus letting opportunities go by.

"One of the problems with what Mark was always doing, and this is one reason when he trained the dentists they did not gel, he was training them to do something that was not going to make them a lot of income right away. They were going to have to fight with the insurance companies about a lot of this. They were paying to be trained and then they were finding out they were going to have to figure out a fee schedule for the calcium therapy. They probably were not real happy. They may have felt they were swindled. On the other hand, what he does is incredibly important to patients," she said.

"What these dentists needed to be told was that you need to look a few years down the road on this because you do these little things now that don't cost the patient a ton of money and you get to save teeth. So when patients need bridges and partials and blah-blah-blah, you keep them as patients with teeth and do their dental work and the patients are happy because they don't have false teeth."

Bonnie confirmed Manhart's contention that dentists in other countries have been generally more receptive to his calcium message than American dentists.

"I did notice when we were in Poland in 1991, for instance, the Polish dentists were with him every step of the way," she said. "There were seventy to eighty dentists, mostly women. There was not the resistance I saw in America, none at all. They had been reading the literature. They had 1950s-era tools and offices but they knew all the literature just exactly as he did and they knew everything he was talking about. They accepted that two plus two equals five."

For Manhart, it was a case of preaching to the choir just like his 2009 presentation at the international dental convention in Spain turned out to be.

Every once in awhile Bonnie said Manhart tries reeling her in again, beseeching her to quit her job in order to assist him with his Calcium Therapy Institute. She lets him know in no uncertain terms that is not happening. "He still asks me to come work for him and his projects, especially when my job is not going so well. I always remind him what a disaster that would be. He cannot promise me there would be money there for benefits and things like that."

Some of Mark and Bonnie's theatre cronies have experienced first hand his magic touch as a dentist. "He is the only dentist I have ever run across that paid any attention to getting my bite right," said Keith Homan. "I have had trouble losing teeth because a dentist would get one bite wrong and then the rest would affect everything else, and I went to him and he got the whole mouth straightened around. He had to do a lot of work to get my teeth to fit, and I have not had any trouble since."

Dave Kistler remembered how Manhart was there for him when he needed him. "I was going to a dentist and one weekend I had this terrible toothache and all they did was give me something for the pain and that did not work out, and I spent one of the most miserable weekends I have ever spent. Then I called Mark and he had me come in and he gave me something to take care of the pain, and that following Monday he worked me into his schedule and took care of my problem."

Those kinds of resolutions are what motivate Manhart to stay in the game, to still come to the office, to see patients, and to say, "Open wide." The term expresses this iconoclast's application of practical, old-fashioned dentistry and open-minded attitudes in adopting new methods as well as the way he openly shares his work and leaves himself wide open to criticism.

It also refers to the wide open aperture he has on life and on all that it offers.

11

Legacy, Contribution, the Journey Continues

There is that basic, fundamental every day dentistry Manhart performs that resolves people's problems. Then, too, there is the matter of legacy, of his discoveries perhaps outliving him. Dental partner Tom Steg said he believes he and Manhart have perhaps made some lasting contributions whose full implications or applications may not be seen until well after they are gone.

"If not in our lifetimes it will be taken over and adopted by somebody and accepted. Maybe that is when periodontists will take it on as their own invention, when he is not around to fight for it," Steg said.

Steg confirmed that Manhart is always searching for ways to broaden the Institute's reach. "He was pursuing and still kind of is pursuing some interest from venture capitalists for an influx of money, which would be a tremendous boon to promote this whole thing. He was close to coming up with something with a couple fellows in that business in California, but they were kind of crooked and he just could not trust them. They were in it just for the money, what they could get out of it, regardless of anything else.

"He is now working with his attorney toward using venture capitalist money to do research at universities. It is one thing going in and asking about doing research, and it is another thing to say I have got a couple hundred thousand dollars here that I would like to coordinate with you for doing some research. Well, then you get something done."

The Calcium Therapy Institute website already has been a boon for making the general public as well as dentists from all over the country, even from all over the world, aware of the alternative treatments available through CTI.

Through much of his struggle to develop new products and treatments Manhart has felt stranded alone on an island, Crusoe-like, with only Steg, in the role of his Man-Friday, as his one professional support. But lately there has been, if not a sea-change, then what Manhart hopes is a rising tide of interest in his work from dentists and MDs. He recently saw a physician he dearly respects who, Manhart said, took time "to explain his changing view of calcium as such an absolute essential to virtually every biological process of the body. His practice interests are leaning more in that direction and the parathyroid gland, the great biological regulator and preservationist. He is smart, I could hardly understand half of his work, and yet he is helping us discover more about cystic therapy."

This fledgling alliance happened like this: When Manhart's severe back problems necessitated surgery some years ago, it was this surgeon who performed the procedure. "He saved my life," Manhart said with no hint of exaggeration; this same surgeon has been coming to Manhart for his dental care. It turned out Manhart diagnosed the cyst problem in him only recently.

"I never really connected it with this because he had no spacing and other symptoms were not evident, except for excess tartar collection on his lower anterior teeth. When I was cleaning his teeth, the tartar was always very difficult to remove."

During that visit the surgeon peeked at the X-rays and Manhart said, "He knew immediately there was something there. He said, 'What's that dark area?' I explained to him about the cyst and I said, 'Do you mind if I treat this area on the upper with calcium, just as a little experiment I want to do?' I wanted to use him as a guinea pig. He laughed and said, 'Sure, I will be your guinea pig.' So I started treating it. When he came in six months later, he had the same tartar in exactly the same place except it was white and it came off easily and that is a characteristic change that occurs when you start treating the cyst. You may still get tartar but it will be white and not colored and not hard."

Then the doctor asked Manhart, "Would this dark mass or void show up in an MRI (Magnetic Resonance Imaging)?' Manhart said, "Absolutely, but I will tell you there would not be a physician or a dentist that would see it because they are so used to seeing it and not seeing it. It is so common." Then the surgeon said, "Yes, but if you showed that it healed that would be entirely different."

Manhart said the physician next surprised him by saying, "'You should have MRIs or CATS taken of this and it would give you confirmation of healing. It would be very, very accurate confirmation of healing.' We both know some radiologists who might help us in doing just that. It is exciting because we can get three-dimensional views that confirm if there is a cyst and that can confirm this whole process of healing."

It is just what Manhart has been hoping might happen. "I figure that even if we got one case of evidence of this healing, it would be confirmation of all that we see in our X-rays and of all the symptoms that we see go away. I have been waiting for over a year for the University of Nebraska to do exactly what this physician brought up. That is a stroke of genius by that guy because that is exactly what should be done. This is what I spent tens of thousands of dollars on to arrange with the university to do. They accepted the whole thing and I have a contract with them to do it and they have done nothing."

Burned by that earlier experience, Manhart has decided he will only work with people and organizations he wants to work with—those who get it and who accept him without condition or reservation. And he is going to get it all in writing before any work is begun. Everything is in place now for a Manhart study that follows patients from the time of diagnosis with the cyst through the entire treatment cycle and on through the healing process and, presumably, the cure. Before, during, and after radiographs are being taken to document the case. Manhart believes he is on the cusp of something big.

"I know this, if you put this on a scale of discoveries, there are very, very few things that have been discovered in dentistry that are more important," he said. "I mean, there are three or four but that's about it and none were discovered in the USA: local anesthesia, high-speed air turbine dental drills, and X-rays are among those, all discovered in Europe. Fluoridation is not as big as ours, which we have uncovered in Omaha, Nebraska, right in the good old USA."

Manhart does not have any plans to check out soon but there are no guarantees in life that he will complete the study or any of the other ambitious goals he has in mind. There is also no guarantee his work will have any lifespan past his own. It is a basic human desire to leave something behind. Beyond the family name that will carry on through his children and their offspring and so forth, there is no doubt that he wants his work to be picked up after he is gone and to be used and advanced for the benefit of generations to come.

He has few provisions in place for that to happen. Of course, this book is a legacy project to a large degree. Besides these pages, he seems to be leaving the fate of his life's work and its perpetuation beyond him up to divine providence, which seems ironic for a man who not only chooses to believe that God is a She but who loves India, a land of countless deities—that is, until you understand he is an independent seeker whose spirituality is strictly a matter between himself and his Higher Power and not the business of any organized religious body.

"Dr. Steg and I have shared virtually everything we have done in our work and I have shared a great deal with my wife," he said, "and between the two of them I do not think this will die, I don't. One of the ways I decided to try to put it out on record was to put it on the Internet. I began to self-publish some of my findings. I have files this long on this subject," he said, spreading his long arms. "It is not comfortable for me to go through those files and this is the reason—there has been so much information that I have tried to promulgate about this, to get dentists to do this ...Tom [Steg] and I used to do seminars, very simple seminars on periodontal therapy and root canal therapy and we would get eight to ten dentists at a time.

"The very fact that dentists would come and listen to us caused so much trouble with specialists that it just got to be more of a hassle then it was worth. This is the kind of thing that led to the court case against me. My work was such a total affront to the specialists. It just goes on and on and on. I still get this claptrap from my colleagues that there is something here that does not work."

He said dental association–dental school indoctrination and peer pressure explain why relatively few American dentists have followed his lead or bothered to learn his calcium therapies. He is training more and more dentists online these days, but they are largely based outside the United States.

Manhart has seen the two-faced nature of the forces opposing him in the States. One side belittles him and his work, casting aspersions that suggest he is a crank and that his theories are unsubstantiated, while the other side obviously recognizes its value and its potential threat to their own work. Attempts have been made to poach and pilfer his calcium therapies. He has tried going through all the proper hoops, barrels, and channels to share his work with colleagues. But playing by the rules has only led to frustration and betrayal.

"I have offered to teach this at the dental schools, and I offered to do all that, and then I found that they were not only stealing my work but they were stealing my patent," he said. "I have a contract to teach, yet I cannot get a job. I start research at my university and I begin what is really important stuff and what I get out of it is, you cannot do that. And I am not getting paid for any of that research. What am

I getting out of this? Nothing. And who is it that wants to stop me? People who could have had it for nothing."

All of which leads Manhart to the conclusion that he has done all he can in this country to have his work validated.

"If it dies that is fine," he said. "I am not being cynical, I am being real. If it dies, it dies. What am I going to do about it? Those who want to continue quarreling and hurting and harming people and doing dumb things that we have found are not necessary, I cannot account for this. A very intelligent guy asked me recently, 'Why is it other dentists don't know about this or don't do this or don't use this?' And I said, 'Well, I cannot account for that, it's not for me to say, because it has been available all these years,' which in a way is the equivalent of saying some day they will have to account for it."

He has resolved not to beat himself up so much about the lost or stolen opportunities for research, saying, "Anymore, I don't care. That's another generation that can take care of that." Surrender is easier said than done.

Everything in its own good time. To everything there is a season. This may all be a case of Manhart being too far out in front of his time. His profession, at least in America, may not have been ready for his message. Or it may be a case of killing the messenger. He may have been the wrong one to advance the calcium therapies because he was not a specialist, because he would not back down or submit, because he insisted on pushing forward in using these therapies and in developing new ones, and because when he did encounter vocal, active resistance, he reacted by not only becoming defensive, even intransigent, but also going on the offensive.

He is perfectly aware that he can come across as arrogant. That he can sound as if he has all the answers. That he portrays himself, perhaps self-servingly, as the White Knight astride his steed slaying the dragons of organized dentistry in his path. That he paints himself the martyr or fall guy taking it on the chin for all the rebels who dare challenge the system. That he claims to be horribly misunderstood, unappreciated, slighted, wronged. Nobody likes a know-it-all, much less a whiner or a whistle blower.

Why would someone who has already troubled the waters, howled at the wind, rattled the cages, and wailed into the night once again tempt fate by articulating for publication, as he does in this treatise, exactly what is on his mind? Why would he risk angering the very powers that be that he says conspire against him? From the perspective of someone who has already boxed himself into a corner, which might describe Manhart's position in the American dental community, he is only left with two choices: quit or come out fighting.

As this book has hopefully established, he is not the quitting type. A good fight suits him just fine, even though he would seem to be badly outnumbered, out-resourced, out-maneuvered to offer little more than token resistance. It is a symbolic fight in truth—in the sense it is one he cannot ultimately win. Organized dentistry will outlast him. It will not endorse him. It will not embrace his theories with open arms. That battle was long ago settled.

But there can be victories by the underdog within the larger war. His real ongoing victory has been in standing up for what he believes and continuing on in spite of the obstacles put in his way—some of his own making. For someone who has lost so much already from his point of view, what else is there to lose? In that light, then, why should he pull any punches? Why not go down fighting? Viewed in the wider scheme of things, who is to say that his calcium therapies will not one day be adopted? That he will not one day be accorded his due?

Of course, there is always the possibility, too, that his calcium therapies are not what he claims or hopes them to be despite the thousands of cases he says that offer evidence to the contrary. But is his work really as important as he suggests? Even he would admit he cannot make a totally reliable appraisal of his own work's worth. Not when so much of him is bound up in it. He is simply too close to it.

Has he really been blackballed by his own profession? It is hard to say when he has burned so many bridges and been caught up in so many disputes. Is he really always the victim or the injured party that he claims to be? Maybe he has just blown disagreements and misunderstandings out of proportion. Maybe he has exaggerated or escalated things to suit his own ends or to support his spin on things. Maybe he has distorted the truth to make himself look good and those he has been in conflict with look bad.

Perhaps instead of people and organizations aligned against him in some kind of conspiracy, each one of his run-ins must be considered on its own merit. There is a context to everything that has happened. Mitigating circumstances may cast a new light on these incidents. Things may not be as black and white or cut and dried as he makes them sound. Perhaps he has been at fault, too. After all, Manhart is only human. His hubris and self-interest cannot help but skew things to some extent.

Undoubtedly, there is another side to the story. But for the purposes of this book, which is not a work of journalism, but an interpretive biography told largely through Manhart's own words, distilled from his own descriptions, veracity is in the eye of the beholder. And so let the reader decide for himself or herself where the truth lies.

In the final analysis, does it really matter what has happened between Manhart and his real or imagined foes? The past is past. All we have is today and maybe the hope of tomorrow.

Besides, as much as Manhart has invested himself in his work, it remains but one aspect of the man. He will never be defined by his dentistry alone. He cannot be so easily or simply understood. His many passions cannot be separated from him or from each other, anymore than one can attend to a single image or shape to the exclusion of every other element in a mural or mosaic. To fully appreciate the whole, one must look at every part. You may not like or understand everything you see, but at least you will have a truer view of all that went into making the man or the artwork. Manhart long ago came to realize that if he were to fulfill his potential, he needed to feed all the different parts of himself. That is how he has lived, and that is the way he will continue to live until the day he dies.

And so he uses his many, varied passions as ballast and balance in his life. "It is very healthy," he said. As long as there is a breath and a spark of life left in him, his ever-searching disposition will be scanning the horizon, like a beacon in the night, looking for the next hill to climb, the next dragon to slay, the next breakthrough to make. Open wide and take in all that life has to offer. Each sweet breath a gift.

He has many miles to go before he rests, but when his time comes, he will be weary from a good long journey that has been full of adventure. The iconoclast will finally sleep. It will be the peaceful sleep of a man who followed his own wide open course.

About the Author

Manhart resides in Omaha, Nebraska with is wife of twenty years, Bonnie Gill. Together they have ten children, eight from Manhart's first marriage, and two from Gill's first marriage. Mark has a thirty-year dental partnership with Dr. Tom Steg.

Exciting things are happening for Mark's Calcium Therapy Institute in the areas of Dentistry and Dermatology all over the world: India, Kathmandu, Brazil, Turkey and from coast to coast.

Praise for
Calcium Therapy Institute

"I began the calcium chips treatments, and instantly—overnight—my sore, aching teeth feel better. (((Smiles)))"

—Dr. Z in Florida

"My teeth and gums are happy, and I really like the Calotion—I also have experienced the cessation of cramping in my legs—and I use it on my face before I apply moisturizing lotions."

—Mo from Colorado

"Dr. Mark, I just wanted to let you know that my teeth and gums never felt so good! I am using the chips about once a week now. Thanks for all your wonderfully productive work and the sincere interest you have in your patients' well being."

—Molly in California

"Dear Dr. M., I have noticed a great difference in my teeth. They seem stronger and whiter—from the inside!"

—Lucy in Arizona

"Hello Doc, My teeth are doing well. I am doing it your calcium way and it's working. Gums are doing good. Thanks!

—S. C. of Tennessee

"Dr. Mark, I just had to write again. Last Friday night, I was bitten by a spider in five different places. One of the bites was close to my underarm. They were large bites and itched like crazy. I put cortisone on them to calm the itching, which worked for four of the five bites; but the one near my underarm not only itched badly, it was painful. The pain expanded from the site of the bite down the left side of my chest. I remembered what you had said about using the Calotion skin lotion on sunburns and how it removed the pain, so I tried it. Within minutes, the itching stopped and within a couple of hours the pain was gone. I continued to use the Calotion on the bite sites for two days just to make sure the inflammation was gone. It was incredible."

—RW in Arizona

"I have been using your products for about a year for burning mouth syndrome. They work wonderfully."

—Charlotte of New York

"Dear CTI, Amazing products! Send more!"

—Gloria in Connecticut

"Hi Dr. M., I have been using the kits for a year now, and my gums feel really great! No problems with my gums, no bleeding, they are firm and nice and pink. Last year my dentist said I had to have gum surgery...this year he didn't mention it! Thank you."

—Paula from New York

"Dear Mark, I have been using your products with astounding results, and not in my mouth. I applied the CZ7 [Calcium Skin Creme] to places my joints have hurt for years, and the pain was gone. And we have your amazing skin solution as well. I want my readers to find out about it."

—Frank in Tennessee

"Thanks! My teeth are doing great! I am continuing to use the chips until my nine-month anniversary date, but they feel like they are much more stable in my mouth than they were before the treatment. Thanks for your help!"

—Brenda in Colorado

"Everyone who has gum disease should contact you first. Calcium Therapy works—surgery is NOT necessary! Thank you. Thank you. Thank you."

—Jerry

"Dear Mark, I have a bone to pick with you: why are you so well hidden? A customer of ours who is a dentist in Mississippi told us about you; otherwise I might never have known about you. My wife had a ferociously itching spot on her shin about the size of an oblong half dollar. Not even iodine was making a dent against it. We put your CZ7 (skin) creme on it and two weeks later it's almost cured. I had keratoderma on my palms and soles that were cured only by massive doses of Vitamin A. It began peeking back on my foot, hands and wrist. Three days on the CZ7 and it is receding. I have no idea what this stuff is, or how it works, but it IS working. I can only imagine what it does for teeth and gums. Why in the world don't more dentists use it?"

—FS in Tennessee

(Dr. Manhart responded with these answers:

Dear FS, We have never hidden our work. We have lectured around the USA and the world and it has been on the Internet since 1995. We've been doing this on patients since 1965. The CZ7 Skin Crème has more health potential than the dental materials, especially in the military. We know what it is, and more than anyone else in the world, how it works. Other dentists will have to account for why they do not know about all this. My account is simple. They have chosen to not know of it. As a result millions of people have suffered.

Best, Dr. Manhart)